The Resistance Cookbook
Nasty Women and Bad Hombres in the Kitchen

By Action Together Massachusetts

Edited by Joan Berglund and Pamela Lowell

Contents

FOREWORD

The Resistance Cookbook: Nasty Women and Bad Hombres in the Kitchen contains all the ingredients for a perfect Resistance Recipe – one that will engage your mind, nourish your body, and lift your soul. Nearly sixty Action Together Massachusetts (ATMA) members contributed their art, humor, and recipes to create a cookbook that will inspire laughter and camaraderie in these challenging times.

Since the 2016 U.S. Presidential election, we have seen a surge of newly impassioned activism. "Nasty women" and "bad hombres" from all walks of life have come together to meet, protest, call, agitate, and activate on behalf of friends, family, neighbors, and the democracy we hold dear.

Action Together Massachusetts was founded in the wake of the 2016 election by women who wanted to work together for a more inclusive, equal, and just United States. Our mission is to empower our members to reclaim their power as voters, constituents, activists, advocates, and allies, and to use the focused strength of our community to affect positive change in the Bay State and beyond.

Fighting for democracy is hard work. We've learned - sometimes the hard way - how important it is to nourish ourselves with both good food and a generous helping of humor. *The Resistance Cookbook* will help on both those fronts. We hope it brings shared smiles with friends and inspires Resistance Potlucks from the pine forests of Maine to the bayous of Florida and all the way across the plains, mesas, and deserts of the country to our fellow resistors on the West Coast.

All proceeds from *The Resistance Cookbook* go directly towards ATMA's work to support and empower the activists who are toiling on the front lines of the Resistance every day. For more information, please visit our websites at www.actiontogetherma.com and www.resistancecookbook.com, and follow us on Twitter

@ActTogetherMA and @ResistCookbook, and on Instagram @ResistanceCookbook.

Contributions to Action Together Massachusetts, Inc. are not tax deductible, but they will make you feel good about contributing to a worthy cause.

#Persist. #Resist. And cook on.

Editor's Note: Joan Berglund

I'm in a lot of vintage kitsch and cookery groups on social media and I noticed an odd trend in the weeks and months following January 20, 2017. A few vintage recipes came up much more frequently than before—Watergate Salad, Watergate Cake, and, of course, Impeachment Icing. It must have been the zeitgeist. Watergate Cake with Impeachment Icing obviously refers to the Nixon scandal, but I wasn't sure about the "salad" (actually pistachio pudding, crushed pineapple and marshmallows). I thought it might be a reference to the hotel. I was wrong; it did refer to the scandal. But in the process of researching, I discovered that there had been a whole cookbook published, *The Watergate Cookbook (Or, Who's in the Soup)*.

With my longstanding interest in twentieth-century history and vintage kitsch (not to mention my newfound interest in impeachment) I decided I had to have my own copy and soon I found one at ABE Books online. It's a funny little book, and it inspired me to start thinking of some of my own recipes: Covfefe Trifle, Flynn's Turkish Tater Toss and China Tried Fried Rice were some early ones. I thought about doing a cookbook on my own, but it seemed like a lot of work for questionable return. I started thinking that it might work better as a group fundraising project.

I posted in my favorite action group, Action Together Massachusetts, and Pamela Lowell and Ruth Chicca and a few others said they would be interested in working on it. We put out a call to the ATMA community and received some great recipes. Molly, an experienced illustrator, volunteered to do the art and Pamela, Ruth and I worked together on the photos. Pamela contributed most of the topical quotes which really added a lot to the project. One of my concerns about *The Watergate Cookbook* was that some of the references were a little obscure 40 years later. With the addition of relevant quotes from our hardworking media outlets, our recipes had context and the book is a little slice of history.

Editor's Note: Pamela Lowell

I first heard about this project through a Facebook post to Action Together Southeastern Massachusetts at the end of June 2017. I had joined several online political groups but hadn't fully committed to any of them. And then there it was! The kernel of an idea, a collection of recipes which would mirror *The Watergate Cookbook* from decades before; a project that would mock the current administration's scandal after scandal; an outlet where I could use all of my political obsession with the never-ending breaking news cycle.

"Let's make it happen," I responded; "Here's a timeline."

What I didn't anticipate was how much fun it would be, what a release it would be from the daily onslaught and trauma of the current regime, or how many new politifriends I would make in the process.

It is important to acknowledge however, that for all of the combined work of Joan Berglund (who had the original idea and did formatting, props and many recipes) and myself (who also edited, came up with quotes, props and photographed) that this was very much a group process from the very beginning.

This was a big huge group project, in fact. With almost 20,000 members in our larger Action Together Massachusetts Facebook Group and the smaller Commission to Write the Cookbook, members decided on the book title, suggested hilarious ideas for the "punny" recipe names and then generously submitted the recipes themselves. They cheered and laughed and responded by tagging each other, and one post alone (with a picture of I'm Still with Her Lasagna) received over 350 ideas and comments! "This is my favorite thread today," someone wrote. "This is my favorite thread ever," another member replied. We all had to agree.

Many thanks to Ruth Chicca for keeping us centered on task when we drifted off course, to Carrie who did our copy editing, to one of our members who kept us accessibility-minded (who is understandably feeling more vulnerable under this current administration), and to Molly for the amazing section title sketches and gorgeous cover art.

We hope that you enjoy reading and cooking from it as much as we did creating it—and that it will inspire you to do your own Action Together.

NOTE ON ABBREVIATIONS

For browsing convenience, we added the following abbreviations to the titles:

GF: gluten-free
OLV: ovo-lacto vegetarian
V: vegan

Please note that none of us are nutritionists, so you'll still need to apply your own judgment to make sure a recipe fits your dietary needs. This is especially true if it includes condiments or other packaged ingredients.

Measurements:

C - cup
lb - pound
oz - ounce
TB - Tablespoon
tsp - teaspoon

APPS AND ALTERNATIVE SNACKS

January 20, 2017   January 21, 2017

WE DON'T GIVE A FIG ABOUT YOUR CROWD SIZE (GF)

Serves 2-4

INGREDIENTS

- 10 to 20 fresh Mission figs (usually find in December)
- Prosciutto (thinly sliced) 1 to 2 slices per fig
- 4 oz package of goat cheese or other soft cheese
- Olive oil

DIRECTIONS

1. Slice fig and stuff with 1 TB cheese.
2. Wrap with 1-2 slices prosciutto and brush lightly with olive oil.
3. Broil for 5-8 minutes until figs are softened and browned.
4. Serve immediately.

Submitted by: Pamela Lowell

"White House counselor Kellyanne Conway claimed that 'alternative facts' were employed by Press Secretary Sean Spicer when he tried to make the case that 'this was the largest audience to ever witness an inauguration, period, both in person and around the globe.'" - Lori Robertson and Robert Farley, "Fact check: The controversy over Trump's inauguration crowd size," *USAToday.com,* January 24, 2017.

ANOTHER CRAB *DIP* IN TRUMP'S APPROVAL RATINGS (GF)

INGREDIENTS

- 2 blocks of cream cheese (softened in microwave for 1 minute approximately)
- 1 1/4 C mayonnaise
- Three 6 oz cans of lump crab meat (drained)
- 1 TB garlic powder
- 1 bunch scallions chopped
- 12 shakes hot sauce

DIRECTIONS

1. Mix all ingredients in a large bowl. Cover and chill for a couple of hours. Serve with crackers, chips, bagels or whatever. Enjoy!

Submitted by: Lee McEvoy Robért

"...Trump's second-quarter job approval rating has fallen below what any other past president has gotten during the same time frame. A new Gallup poll found that Trump aver-

aged a 38.8% rating between April 20 and July 19. The average approval rating for that time is 62%." - Tessa Berenson, "President Trump's Approval Rating Is Worse Than Any Other President At This Point," *Time.com,* July 21, 2017.

"Donald J. Trump's approval rating of 37 is significant because it is a record low and also because it is his IQ." - Andy Borowitz, *Facebook.com*, March 19, 2017.

DONALD'S SMALL PICKLES (REFRIGERATED SWEET AND SOUR) (GF, V)

Serves 2-4

INGREDIENTS

- 3 C cucumbers sliced
- 1 C apple cider vinegar
- 1 C white balsamic vinegar
- 1/4 C honey or agave syrup
- 1/4 tsp celery seed
- 1/4 tsp red chili flakes (or dill)
- 1/4 tsp salt

DIRECTIONS

1. In pan over medium-high heat, add all ingredients except for cucumbers.
2. Heat and stir together until blended well. Let cool for 10-15 minutes.
3. Put cucumbers in jar (Ball jar or other glass container).
4. Pour liquid over cucumbers and refrigerate for 24-48 hours before serving.

Submitted by Pamela Lowell

"'And he referred to my hands—if they're small something else must be small,' [Trump said]". - Gregory Krieg, "Donald Trump defends size of his penis," *CNN.com*, March 4, 2016.

"I guarantee you, I've plowed many fields with my peanut," President Jimmy Carter (not really). - Peter Allen Clark, "6 presidential quotes about penis size that Donald Trump would endorse," *Mashable.com*, March 3, 2016.

CREATE YOUR OWN YELLOW PUFFED CHEESE FLAVORED SNACK RECIPE (OLV)

Buy a package of your favorite Yellow Puffed Cheese-Flavored Snack (YPCFS) and use it to make any of the following:

Nothing Burger (topped with YPCFS and a side of Bob Mueller's Dream Team)

Macaroni and Cheese topped with. . . YPCFS!

Grilled Cheese Sandwiches (bread, cheese, YPCFS)

Broccoli with YPCFS (or any vegetable that needs a crunchy kick)

Submitted by: Anonymous

"Q. Why is Trump sometimes referred to as the Orange Cheeto [registered trademark]?

A.' Because he used to sport what looked like an awful spray tan that made him look orange. It really doesn't apply anymore as it appears he has foregone using it. He is now his real pink-white color, kind of like a naked mole rat.'

B. 'Because his hair is the color of the artificial chemical coloring in Cheetos [registered trademark] and he cheats a lot'" -comments on *answers.yahoo.com*, September 2, 2017.

HILLA-BRIE (OLV)

INGREDIENTS

- One 7 oz box of frozen puff pastry, thawed
- 8 oz round of brie cheese
- 1/4 C almond slices, toasted
- 1/4 C raspberry preserves (or, use flavor of your choice)
- 1 egg, beaten

DIRECTIONS

1. Preheat oven to 425 degrees Fahrenheit.
2. Lightly grease cookie sheet (or place parchment paper on cookie sheet).
3. Roll one sheet of pastry out.

4. Leaving rind on brie, spread preserves on side and top of brie, sprinkle almonds on top.
5. Place pastry on brie, then turn over and gather the pastry together and press together so brie is encased, making sure it's tucked neatly together so jam won't seep out when cooked.
6. Turn brie over, so untucked side is on top.
7. Cut decorative design out of remaining sheet of pastry, place on top.
8. Brush with beaten egg.
9. Cook for about 25 minutes, until golden and let sit for 5 minutes.
10. Serve with crackers, sliced apples and pears.

CONTRIBUTOR NOTES

Hillary's logo is the perfect Hilla-brie decoration! I made this for the first Clinton/Trump debate, and we devoured it while we cheered her on and hissed at him....

Submitted by: Margot

"In a relentlessly antagonistic debate, Donald J. Trump and Hillary Clinton clashed over trade, the Iraq War, his refusal to release his tax returns and her use of a private email server, with Mr. Trump frequently showing impatience and political inexperience as Mrs. Clinton pushed him to defend his past denigration of women and President Obama." - Patrick Healy and Jonathan Martin, "Hillary Clinton and Donald Trump Press Pointed Attacks in Debate," *NYTimes.com,* September 26, 2016.

"The visual - the split screen - of Donald Trump looming over Hillary Clinton, pacing around, leaning on the chair was very strange....He spent an entire debate saying absolutely nothing about the issues he was asked about...but when he did get specific, he admitted to not paying federal taxes...even when confronted with the fact that this means he did not contribute to funding our military, to funding our veterans administration, to funding roads and bridges and

infrastructure and all the rest.... It was a stunning debate that would have been much more fitting in the third world than it was in the United States of America." - Joy Reid, "Reid: Trump represented a type of 'thugocracy,'" *MSNBC.com*, October 9, 2016.

PROTEST MARCH PORTABLE GRANOLA (V)

INGREDIENTS

- 3 C oats
- 1 C whole wheat flour
- 1/3 C vegetable oil
- 2/3 C maple syrup
- 1 tsp vanilla extract
- Pinch of salt
- 1 C seeds and nuts
- 1 tsp cinnamon, nutmeg, allspice, or ground ginger or some combination of these
- 1 C dried fruit of your choice

DIRECTIONS

1. Pre-heat oven to 350 degrees Fahrenheit.
2. In large bowl, mix dry ingredients.
3. Add wet ingredients.
4. Stir together well.
5. Turn out to shallow baking sheet lined with parchment paper.
6. Bake for 20-25 minutes, stirring and rotating baking sheet every so often and checking for doneness.
7. Remove from oven, break up large pieces and cool.
8. Add dried fruit. This is a very adaptable recipe. It can be doubled easily. Gluten-free ingredients can be substituted.

CONTRIBUTOR NOTES

My first yoga teacher gave me this recipe and I think of her every time I make it.

Submitted by: Stephanie Gibbs

"The Women's March was a worldwide protest on January 21, 2017, to advocate legislation and policies regarding human rights and other issues, including women's rights, immigration reform, healthcare reform, reproductive rights, the natural environment, LGBTQ rights, racial equality, freedom of religion, and worker's rights. Most of the rallies were aimed at Donald Trump…. It was the largest single-day protest in U.S. history." - Wikipedia, "2017 Women's March https://en.wikipedia.org/wiki/2017_Women%27s_March, last modified October 30, 2017.

"Crowd Scientists say Women's March in Washington had 3 times as many people as Trump's Inauguration." - Tim Wallace and Alicia Parlapiano, *NYTimes.com,* January 22, 2017.

MITCH MCCONNELL IS THE DEVILED EGGS (GF, OLV)

Makes 12

INGREDIENTS

- 1 dozen eggs
- 2 to 3 TB mayo
- 2 to 3 TB mustard
- 1 to 2 TB green relish
- 1 to 2 caps full of white vinegar
- Sea salt
- Paprika

DIRECTIONS

1. Hard boil a dozen eggs. Wait until they are completely cooled (soak them in ice water or leave them in the fridge) and then peel the eggs.
2. Cut the eggs in half and scoop out the yolk. Put all the yolks into a medium-sized mixing bowl.
3. Mash the yolks with the mayo, mustard, and relish. It's better to start with smaller amounts of the wet ingredients and slowly add more until you have the consistency and taste that you like. If you add more mayo and mustard the final mixture will be runnier; less and the mixture will be drier. The type of mayo and mustard you use (yellow vs. spicy brown, for instance) will also impact the final flavor. Combine the yolks with the mayo, mustard, green relish, and white vinegar until fully mixed.
4. Scoop the mixture back into the emptied egg whites.
5. Sprinkle with sea salt (use a light hand).
6. Cover with paprika. Enjoy!

Submitted by: S. Wright

"The single most important thing we want to achieve is for President Obama to be a one-term president." - Senate Minority Leader Mitch McConnell, quoted in *National Journal,* November 4, 2010.

"What I find most offensive about McConnell is the astonishing heights of hypocrisy that he wields like a sledgehammer. The shamelessness of McConnell's hypocrisy is only matched by the shamelessness of Donald Trump's lying and that's really saying something." - Justin Rosario, "It's Hard Not To Hate Mitch McConnell," *TheDailyBanter.com*, April 6, 2017.

MAN-GO CRAZY SALSA (GF, V)

INGREDIENTS

- 1 mango, diced
- 1 large tomato, diced
- 1 red onion, diced
- Juice from 1/2 of lime
- 1 jalapeno, minced
- 1/4 C chopped fresh cilantro
- Dash of salt

DIRECTIONS

1. Prepare the ingredients and combine in bowl. Add salt to taste. Serve with tortilla chips & a side of "unpresidented" crazy.

Submitted by: Wendy Reclaiming Time

"I watched President Trump's news conference the other day, and I thought: He's kind of crazy. Not crazy crazy. But you know, just weird." - Robin Abcarian, "President Trump is a 'world class narcissist,' but he's not mentally ill, says the psychiatrist who helped define narcissism," *LATimes.com*, February 19, 2017.

"I began my day today as I often begin my days by checking Donald Trump's Twitter feed to see how far the crazy has spread," Colbert said. *"Today, I really think he's off his meds because today he went from crazy to cruel."* - Stephen Colbert on Trump's Transgender Ban, *The Late Show*, July 26, 2017.

KALE-Y-ANNE'S ALTERNATIVE CHIPS (GF, V)

INGREDIENTS

- 2 C of kale, washed, stemmed and torn into chip-sized pieces
- Salt, garlic salt or other seasoned salt
- Best quality extra-virgin olive oil

DIRECTIONS

1. Put the kale in a casserole dish with a cover or in a plastic bag. Drizzle with olive oil and sprinkle with your seasonings. Shake well to coat all the leaves.
2. Line a baking sheet with foil or parchment paper sprayed with olive oil spray and spread the kale thinly on it.
3. Put into a cold oven and then set the temperature for 350 degrees Fahrenheit.
4. Check the kale when the oven comes to temperature, in about 10 minutes. It probably will still need another 5-10 minutes. Check every couple of minutes and take them out when they are fully dried and just barely starting to brown.
5. Use a thin spatula to carefully loosen them from the sheet or let them cool a little and use your hands. They will be a little fragile compared to potato chips, so I find the best way to get them off the pan is to make a funnel out of the foil or paper and carefully pour them.

CONTRIBUTOR NOTES

I like to use freshly ground sea salt and spice mixes with garlic or hot pepper and serve with a grilled cheese sandwich and tomato soup.

Submitted by: Joan Berglund

"Stelter: 'The scandals are about the President's lies. About voter fraud, about wiretapping, his repeated lies about those issues. That's the scandal.'

Conway: '(Donald Trump) doesn't think he's lying about those issues and you know it.'" - Chris Cillizza, "Kellyanne Conway offers alternative fact to explain why Trump isn't lying," *CNN.com*, July 24, 2017.

DEBATE CELERY STALKING WITH CRANBERRIES AND GOAT CHEESE (GF, OLV)

INGREDIENTS

- Celery stalks (cut in thirds)
- One package goat cheese
- Chopped walnuts (or pecans)
- Dried cranberries

DIRECTIONS

1. Spread goat cheese onto celery stalks.
2. Sprinkle with walnuts and dried cranberries.

CONTRIBUTOR NOTES

This is a nice easy appetizer for dinner parties made with things you might already have in the kitchen. Make sure you're around like-minded adults though so that you won't have to tell them to "BACK UP, YOU CREEP!"

Submitted by: Still With Her

"Do you stay calm, keep smiling and carry on as if he weren't repeatedly invading your space? Or do you turn, look him in the eye and say loudly and clearly, 'Back up, you creep. Get away from me. I know you love to intimidate women, but you can't intimidate me, so back up.'" - Hillary Clinton, *What Happened*, (New York: Simon & Schuster, 2017).

RESOURCEFUL BROTH (GF, V)

INGREDIENTS

- Vegetable scraps, washed and stored in freezer (this includes, but isn't limited to, carrot, onion and potato peelings, celery tops, broccoli or kale stems, asparagus or green beans ends, mushrooms, peppers, scallions, scraps, leftover lettuce or chard, etc.)
- Your favorite fresh herbs (parsley, basil, thyme, oregano, rosemary, marjoram, fennel, bay leaf)
- 14 to 16 C of water
- Salt and pepper to taste

DIRECTIONS

1. As you make your meals over the course of a week or month, save all the vegetable scraps you can in an air-tight gallon freezer zip-lock bag. Scraps can be saved for up to a month in the freezer. Note: if you're in a hurry and don't have any scraps, you can make this broth using whole vegetables, simply chop in chunks for easier cooking.
2. When you have a bag filled with vegetables, remove it from the freezer to make your broth.
3. In a large sauce pan, bring 14 to 16 C of water to a boil.
4. Once boiling, add all the scraps from the gallon freezer bag.
5. Add your favorite fresh herbs, and garlic if you enjoy.
6. Season with salt and pepper.
7. Bring to a boil, then lower to a simmer, stirring occasionally.
8. Simmer the broth for 30 minutes.
9. Using a slotted spoon, remove the larger vegetable scraps from the broth and discard. Next, strain the broth through a fine-meshed strainer or colander lined with cheesecloth. Carefully pour the broth

through the strainer into another pot. Discard - or compost! - remaining scraps, veggies and herbs.

10. Allow broth to cool completely (about 1-2 hours).
11. Broth can be stored in the fridge for up to 1 week, frozen for up to 3 months, or canned with proper canning techniques. If freezing, recommend freezing in 2- to 4- C increments (and writing the quantity on the packaging) so you know the quantity when you're ready to defrost and use.

CONTRIBUTOR NOTES

From scraps that would typically be thrown away, here we make a delicious and nutritious vegetable broth. This broth can be used as the base for any soup you make, or as its own healing soup, perhaps with some fresh veggies or noodles. In this broth, we are being resourceful and using all of a vegetable, even the parts that would typically be thrown out. Wasting not is a way to honor to the environment, the beautiful vegetables we grow and consume, and is a sign that being resourceful and scrappy can feed bodies and souls.

Submitted by: Carrie M.

"Up to 40 percent of food in the United States goes uneaten. That is on average 400 pounds of food per person every year. Not only is that irresponsible - it's expensive.... Wasted food is also a major contributor to climate change, producing more greenhouse gas emissions than 37 million cars.... In fact, food is the number one contributor to landfills today." - Dana Gunders, "Wasted: How America Is Losing Up to 40 Percent of Its Food from Farm to Fork to Landfill," *NRDC.org*, August 16, 2017.

"That a misogynist perpetrator of violence could still lead and represent our nation, and that a massive number of Americans will still vote for him despite these revelations, is infuriating. For women who have endured harassment, for those who have been silenced by a man's power, and for survivors of abuse or sexual assault, the tenor of this reckon-

ing can be exhausting and triggering. It requires self-care."
- Julie Zeilinger, "Self-Care in the Time of Trump," *MTV.com*, October 13, 2017.

SOMETHING FISHY IN THE WHITE HOUSE CHOW-DA (GF)

INGREDIENTS

- Container of fresh clams (seafood department) could also use shrimp/haddock/flounder
- 1 small potato peeled and diced small pieces
- 2 to 3 scallions chopped
- 1 stalk celery chopped very fine
- 1 can coconut milk (GF) or Carnation Evaporated Milk (not sweetened condensed)

DIRECTIONS

1. Simmer potatoes and scallions and celery in small amount of water (just to cover it about one inch) in sauce pan.
2. When potatoes are tender add clams and simmer 5-10 minutes on low until clams are how you like them (not tough).
3. Add can of Carnation Milk or coconut milk and bring to heat thoroughly (but watch it so it doesn't boil).
4. Enjoy a cup of New England.

Submitted by: Pamela Lowell

"'The fish rots, again from the head,' [Joe] Scarborough said. 'At what point do Republicans start criticizing Donald Trump for attacking federal judges? At what point do Republicans start criticizing Donald Trump for using a Stalinist trick, calling the press enemies of the people?'" - Travis Gettys, "'The fish rots from the head': Morning Joe blames 'brutish' Trump for Gianforte's assault on reporter," *RawStory.com*, May 25, 2017.

COMEY TESTIMONY MINESTRONE
(Complicated but worth the wait)

INGREDIENTS

- 2 cans whole tomatoes
- 1 lb ground meat (for meatballs, or use vegan meat-balls)
- 1 can kidney beans (or any beans you desire)
- 1 onion chopped
- 1 bunch parsley chopped
- 1 head cabbage (must be green) chopped
- 1 box spaghetti (I use GF)
- 2 to 3 beef bouillon cubes

- Freshly grated Parmesan cheese

DIRECTIONS

1. Make small meatballs using ground meat and chopped onion and bake for 20 minutes at 350 (or use prepared meatballs).
2. Add meatballs and canned tomatoes in large pot. Add 4 to 6 C water and simmer for one hour.
3. Add kidney beans, parsley, cabbage, and bouillon cubes to minestrone and simmer until cabbage is tender approximately 15 minutes.
4. In the meantime, prepare one box spaghetti according to package directions.
5. Put a serving size of spaghetti into each individual bowl and spoon minestrone over spaghetti.
6. Generously heap Parmesan cheese.

Submitted by: Pamela Lowell

"I was alone with the president-elect...I was honestly concerned he might lie about the nature of our meeting so I thought it important to document. That combination of things I had never experienced before led me to believe I got to write it down and write it down in a very detailed way." - James B. Comey, former Director of the FBI, in prepared testimony submitted to the Senate Select Committee on Intelligence, June 8, 2017.

ALT-CLAM CHOWDER (V, GF)

INGREDIENTS

Mushrooms

- 1 TB vegan butter (or extra virgin olive oil)
- 8 oz white button mushrooms, cut into 1/2 inch pieces (or any mushrooms)
- 1 garlic clove, minced
- 1 tsp low sodium tamari (or soy sauce)

"Cream" Sauce

- 1 C cauliflower, slightly steamed
- 3/4 C nondairy milk
- 1 TB vegan butter
- 1/4 tsp kosher salt plus more to taste
- 1/4 tsp cracked pepper

Soup Base

- 1/2 medium yellow onion, diced
- 2 celery stalks, rinsed & finely diced
- 3 medium-sized carrots, diced
- 1/3 C frozen corn
- 1 tsp dried thyme or 5 to 6 fresh thyme sprigs
- 3 TB gluten-free flour (or all-purpose flour if you don't have GF)
- 1 medium Yukon Gold potato, washed and cut into 3/4 inch cubes
- 3 C low-sodium vegetable broth
- 1/2 C nondairy milk
- 1/4 C fresh parsley, chopped

Optional Garnish

- 2 TB fresh parsley, chopped
- Oyster crackers
- Sliced button mushrooms

DIRECTIONS

Mushrooms

1. Heat the 1 TB butter (or extra virgin olive oil) in a large saucepan over medium heat.
2. When melted, add the mushrooms and sauté over medium high heat. Stir occasionally and cook until the liquid evaporates (about 3 minutes).
3. Add garlic and tamari (or soy sauce).
4. Sauté until the mushrooms are tender and lightly browned (about 3 minutes). Note: while mushrooms are cooking, you can begin steaming the cauliflower for the "Cream" Sauce.
5. Remove mushrooms from heat and set aside.

"Cream" Sauce

1. Slightly steam the cauliflower.
2. Blend all the "cream" sauce ingredients together in a high-speed blender. If it is too thick to blend, add one TB of nondairy milk at a time until desired consistency. Adjust salt and pepper seasoning according to preference.

Soup base

1. Sauté the onions, celery, carrots, corn, and thyme together over medium-high heat until the onions are translucent, stirring occasionally.
2. Add the flour and mix until well-combined.
3. Add the broth and nondairy milk. Bring to a boil, stirring constantly.
4. Add the chopped potatoes and cream base. Bring to a boil, then reduce heat. Simmer until potatoes are tender (about 10-15 minutes).
5. Add the sautéed mushrooms and chopped parsley. Heat another 2-3 minutes.
6. Season according to taste. If you used sprigs of thyme, remove them.

7. Ladle the soup into bowls and garnish with fresh parsley.

CONTRIBUTOR NOTES

Make it soy free: Use coconut aminos instead of tamari or soy sauce. Make it gluten-free: Verify that your tamari and flour is gluten-free.

Submitted by: Carrie M.

"The earliest-established and most popular variety of clam chowder, New England clam chowder, was introduced to the region by French, Nova Scotian or British settlers, becoming common in the 18th century. In 1939, the New England State of Maine debated legislation that would outlaw the use of tomatoes in chowder, thereby essentially prohibiting the 'Manhattan' form. - Wikipedia, "Clam Chowder," last modified September 12, 2017, https://en.wikipedia.org/wiki/ Clam_chowder.

TRUMPKIN SEAFOOD CHOWDER (GF)

INGREDIENTS

Serves 4

- 1/2 lb firm white fish such as cod or haddock cut into bite-sized pieces
- 3/4 lb assorted fresh seafood or thawed frozen blend (Trader Joe's is one brand)
- Two 8 oz bottles of clam juice or 2 C of seafood broth
- 1 medium potato, chopped
- 1 medium onion, diced
- 1 clove of garlic, finely diced
- One 11 oz can of plain pureed pumpkin (NOT pumpkin pie filler) or 1 1/2 C pureed roasted pumpkin
- 2 TB olive or vegetable oil
- Dash of sherry or wine (optional)
- Salt and pepper to taste

DIRECTIONS

1. Heat the olive oil in your soup pan on medium heat, add diced onions and cook for 5-7 minutes until they start to soften. Add the garlic and cook for an additional 30 seconds.
2. Add the clam juice (and wine if using) and the potatoes and bring it to a boil.
3. Reduce heat to a simmer and cook until the potatoes and onions are soft, about 10 minutes.
4. Add the white fish and simmer for about 3-5 minutes until almost cooked through.
5. Add the seafood and cook an additional 3-5 minutes until just cooked through.
6. Add the pumpkin and heat for an additional minute or two until it's heated through. Add salt and pepper to taste.

CONTRIBUTOR NOTES

Cooking times depend on the exact seafood you choose, so use your judgment and be careful not to overcook. This recipe can be as fussy or as lazy as you want as far as choosing fresh or packaged ingredients. You can garnish with pan-fried sage leaves or a swirl of cream or sour cream, although I think it has plenty of richness without dairy.

Submitted by: Joan Berglund

"Trumpkin: A supporter of Donald Trump's candidacy for the Presidency of the United States of America; the term invokes the munchkins of Oz, a minitiarized [sic] people of questionable intellectual backing and strong propensity towards astronomical heights of gullibility. Note: While the term can be used to describe any Trump supporter, it is usually reserved for either his online trolls or surrogates. It is rarely used in reference to his rallygoers, who are most often referred to as Trumpa Loompas." - "Trumpkin," *Urband-Dictionary.com*, accessed October 7, 2017, https://www.urbandictionary.com/define.php?term=Trumpkin.

GOLDEN SHOWER GAZPACHO (GF, V)

INGREDIENTS

Serves 4 as an appetizer

- 3 large yellow heirloom tomatoes, cut in large chunks (or 2 pints yellow grape or cherry tomatoes)
- 2-inch piece of sweet onion
- 1 clove garlic
- 1/2 English cucumber, peeled and quartered
- 1/2 yellow pepper
- 1 tsp extra virgin olive oil
- 1 tsp white balsamic vinegar

DIRECTIONS

7. In a food processor, blend 1/3 of tomatoes.

8. Gradually add onion and garlic, blend until smooth.
9. Pour into medium bowl.
10. In food processor, blend remaining tomatoes, cucumber, pepper, olive oil, vinegar.
11. Combine all components in the bowl and stir.
12. Salt, pepper, and additional oil and vinegar to taste.

CONTRIBUTOR NOTES

Serve in small bowls with spoons or in martini glasses and drink. Some diced avocado on top makes a lovely garnish. Perfect when you're having company, from Russian escorts to former British intelligence officers.

Submitted by: Joyce Johns and Kate Raftery

"What is in the dossier? Well it includes a wealth of information about a series of possible meetings... It's the pee pee tape, it talks about the pee pee tape. What New Yorker would travel 2000 miles to watch someone pee? It's free on the L Train." - Stephen Colbert, *The Late Show with Stephen Colbert*, October 16, 2017.

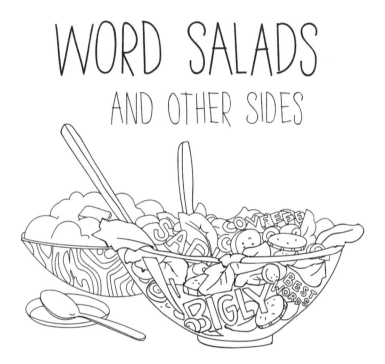

BOWLING GREEN SALAD
(*With Never Remember Croutons*)

Serves 4-6

INGREDIENTS

- 2 C chopped raw spinach
- 2 C chopped romaine
- 1 avocado, pitted peeled and chopped
- 1 cucumber, peeled and cubed
- 1/4 C diced tomatoes
- 1/4 C protein of your choice (I suggest bacon!)
- 1/4 C shredded cheese of your choice
- 1 loaf French bread
- Olive oil
- Salt and pepper.
- 2 TB minced garlic

DIRECTIONS

Salad:

1. Mix greens and salad toppings and toss together in your favorite dressing (like a vinaigrette). Salt and pepper to taste.

Never Remember Croutons:

1. Cube and toss bread in olive oil and minced garlic. Bake for approximately 10 minutes or until crispy, tossing frequently.

CONTRIBUTOR NOTES

I make the best salads. Tremendous salads. Everyone says so. Big, huge salads.

Submitted by: Stephanie Roberts

"I bet it's brand-new information to people that President Obama had a six-month ban on the Iraqi refugee program after two Iraqis came here to this country, were radicalized and were the masterminds behind the Bowling Green massacre. Most people don't know that because it didn't get covered." - Kellyanne Conway on *Hardball with Chris Matthews*, February 2, 2017.

"WRONG." - Daniel Pike, "Trump adviser falsely references BG 'massacre,'" *Bowling Green Daily News*, February 3, 2017.

"The Bowling Green massacre didn't get covered because it didn't happen." - Lindsey Bever, "Kellyanne Conway cites 'Bowling Green massacre' that never happened to defend travel ban," *WashingtonPost.com*, February 3, 2017.

WA-PO TATO SALAD (GF)
Because mayonnaise dies in darkness

Serves 4-6

INGREDIENTS

- 2-3 lb gold Yukon potatoes, cut in half with salt and pepper
- Bacon, one package chopped
- 1 red onion, diced
- 1 small green pepper, chopped small
- 1 TB smoked paprika
- 1/4 C fresh parsley, chopped
- 2 cloves garlic, diced (optional)

Dressing

- 1/4 C red wine vinegar
- 1 TB oregano
- 1 tsp brown sugar
- Salt and pepper
- 1 to 2 TB capers

DIRECTIONS

1. Preheat oven to 425 degrees Fahrenheit. Grease baking dish with olive oil.
2. Add potatoes (cut side down in pan) and roast for 45 minutes to 1 hour. When finished cooking, remove and cut into bite-sized pieces.
3. In frying pan cook bacon and drain. In some of the bacon fat, cook red onion, pepper and garlic (if using) until translucent.
4. Add paprika and parsley for last few minutes.
5. In large bowl combine potatoes, bacon, onion, pepper and dressing. Serve warm.

Submitted by: Warren Lowell, Humphrey School of Public Affairs '19

"As the Trump administration unfolds, it seems like a new bombshell story breaks every other day. Chances are the writers behind those stories come from either The Washington Post or The New York Times." - The Leonard Lopate Show, "The Unexpected Battle Between The Washington Post & The New York Times," *WNYC.com*, August 23, 2017.

"There is no more important struggle for American democracy than ensuring a diverse, independent and free media. Free Press is at the heart of that struggle." - Bill Moyers

"They say "democracy dies in darkness". The truth is, democracy gets stabbed in the front, back and in the face whenever Republicans are in charge of any legislature. What a hypocritical bunch of criminals, thugs and scam artists they are. #TaxScamBill." - @AshaDahya, *Twitter.com*, December 2, 2017.

NORTH AND SOUTH MAPLE CORNBREAD (OLV)

Serves 9 to 16

INGREDIENTS

- 1 C whole wheat flour
- 1 C yellow corn meal
- 1 TB baking powder
- 1/2 tsp kosher salt
- 1 C milk
- 1/4 C maple syrup
- 4 TB butter, melted and allowed to cool slightly
- 2 whole eggs

DIRECTIONS

1. Preheat oven to 425 degrees Fahrenheit. Grease a nonstick 8x8 pan.
2. In a large mixing bowl, whisk flour, cornmeal, baking powder, and salt.
3. In a smaller bowl, whisk milk, maple syrup, butter, and eggs.
4. Add the liquid ingredients to the dry ingredients and gently stir until just moistened. Don't over stir!
5. Pour batter into prepared pan and bake 20-25 minutes, or until golden brown and a toothpick inserted in the middle comes out clean.

Submitted by: Rachel Trousdale

"I believe this Government cannot endure, permanently, half slave and half free. I do not expect the Union to be dissolved—I do not expect the house to fall—but I do expect it will cease to be divided." -Abraham Lincoln, House Divided Speech, June 16, 1858.

PEES AND SHALLOTS (GF, OLV)

Serves 4

INGREDIENTS

- Your favorite canned, frozen or fresh peas
- 1 shallot, chopped fine
- Good olive oil
- Butter

DIRECTIONS

1. Heat a skillet and add 2 TB of butter and drizzle olive oil allow to melt and heat.
2. Add shallot to hot oil and cook until tender and soft.
3. Add peas.
4. Heat through stirring constantly until hot.
5. Serve.

CONTRIBUTOR NOTES

This is a simple recipe, but really tasty.

Submitted by: Ann-Mary Spellman

"The Donald-Trump-Russia dossier is a private intelligence dossier that was written by Christopher Steele, a former British MI6 intelligence officer." - Wikipedia, "Donald Trump–Russia dossier," last modified October 30, 2017, https://en.wikipedia.org/wiki/Donald_Trump%E2%80%93Russia_dossier.

"'Now, the wildest accusations in that dossier have never been confirmed," Steve Colbert said, but as he believes, "It's the part we talk about, the pee-pee tape." After searching the streets for the alleged footage, he went inside the suite. "When you're in this room, I don't know how to describe it," Colbert mused. "It's soaked in history.'" - Erin Jenson, "'Late Show: Stephen Colbert searches for alleged Trump 'pee-pee tape,'" *USAToday.com,* July 21, 2017.

RADICALLY GOOD SYRIAN TABOULI SALAD (V)

Serves 4 to 6

INGREDIENTS

- 1/2 C dry cracked wheat/ bulgur wheat (#1)
- 2 large bunches fresh parsley, de-stemmed and finely chopped (about 2 to 3 C finely chopped)
- 1 large bunch fresh mint, de-stemmed and finely chopped (about 1 C finely chopped)
- 1 bunch of scallions, finely chopped
- 3 to 4 large finely diced tomatoes (about 3 C)
- 1/3 C light olive oil or corn oil
- Juice of 2 large lemons
- 1 tsp salt (approximately)
- Dash allspice
- Dash cinnamon

DIRECTIONS

1. Soak cracked wheat in warm water for about 1/2 hour.
2. Mix the parsley, mint, scallions, tomatoes, lemon juice and oil.
3. Drain the cracked wheat well, squeezing out and discarding excess water with hands.
4. Add the drained wheat to the tomatoes mixture; add a dash of allspice and a dash of cinnamon.
5. Add approximately 1 tsp salt or to taste and mix.
6. Refrigerate for approximately an hour, adjust seasoning to taste. Serve with lettuce leaves or pita bread if desired.

CONTRIBUTOR NOTES

Traditionally garnished with a sprig of mint and lemon wedges. Served with pita bread or whole lettuce leaves. Vegetarian, low fat.

Each Lebanese or Syrian family seems to have its own spin on tabouli. This was my Sitto's (grandma's) recipe. Some may prefer more wheat, more parsley, etc. Feel free to adjust proportions as you see fit. Eating this dish does not necessarily result in becoming radicalized.

Submitted by: Alicia Rinaldi

"The Syrian refugees who are coming to the US are among the most vulnerable in the Syrian conflict: many are women and their children, religious minorities and victims of violence and torture." - Lauren Gambino, "Trump and Syrian refugees in the US: separating the facts from fiction," *TheGuardian.com*, September 2, 2016.

"US to Ban Syrian Refugees, Israel accepts 100 Syrian Orphans." - David Israel, *Jewish-Press.com*, January 26, 2017.

MEXICO WILL PAY FOR THE WALL-DORF SALAD (OLV)

Serves 4 to 6

INGREDIENTS

- 3 tsp lime juice
- 1 1/2 C of water
- 1 1/2 lb large red apples
- 3/4 C chopped celery
- 2/3 C raisins
- 1/2 C chopped jicama
- 3/4 C Mexican crema or sour cream
- 3 TB mayonnaise
- 1 pinch salt and pepper
- Maraschino cherries and curly parsley for garnish

DIRECTIONS

1. Add the lime juice to the water in a large bowl and set aside.

2. Core and chop the apples, leaving the skin on for color.
3. Toss the apples into the lime water.
4. Drain the apples.
5. Add celery, jicama and raisins to the apples.
6. Mix the crema or sour cream in a small bowl with the mayonnaise.
7. Add mayonnaise mixture, salt and pepper over the fruit and stir to combine.
8. Chill for 1 hour in the refrigerator or until ready to serve.
9. Garnish with cherries and parsley.

CONTRIBUTOR NOTES

This is a nut-free version, but feel free to add 2/3 C chopped pecans or walnuts as desired.

Submitted by: Ruth Chicca

"Former Mexican President Vicente Fox is making his position clear on Donald Trump's pledge to make Mexico pay for a wall along the U.S.-Mexico border. 'I'm not going to pay for that f'ing wall. He should pay for it,'" - Tom LoBianco, "Ex-Mexican president Fox: 'I'm not going to pay for that f'ing wall,'" *CNN.com*, February 25, 2016.

FAKE NEWDLES SPIRALIZER CAPRESE SALAD (GF, OLV)

Serves 2 as a main dish or 4 as a side

INGREDIENTS

- 4 oz small fresh mozzarella balls (1-inch diameter)
- 2 medium zucchinis or summer squashes
- 2 C cherry or grape tomatoes (mixed heirloom varieties if you can get them)
- 2 TB fresh basil, sliced thin
- Salt and pepper to taste
- 1 TB good extra-virgin olive oil or to taste
- 1 TB good balsamic vinegar or to taste

DIRECTIONS

1. Halve the mozzarella balls. If your tomatoes are on the larger side, halve or quarter them as well.
2. Cut whole zucchinis into sections of about 2 inches. The size of the sections will determine the length of your zoodles. Process each section on the B blade if you have a spiralizer that has multiple blades. Refer to the instructions for your device for more details.
3. Gently toss all ingredients except for oil and vinegar.
4. Drizzle with the oil and vinegar. Toss again to combine or leave it as a decorative drizzle depending on your preference.

Submitted by: Joan Berglund

"Jimmy Kimmel used CNN's Wolf Blitzer to show the three ways you can tell when something is 'fake news' 1) It's mean to President Trump; 2) It's negative; and 3) That's it. He then used Fox & Friends to show the three ways you can tell when something is Fox News: 1) It's nice to President Trump; 2) It's positive; and 3) It has nothing to do with anything!" - Joseph A. Wulfsohn, "Fake News vs Fox News:

Jimmy Kimmel Guides Viewers On How to Tell the Difference," *MediaITE.com*, May 18, 2017.

LOVE IS LOVE RAINBOW MOSAIC SALAD (V or OLV)

Serves 4 to 6

INGREDIENTS

- 1 package mixed salad greens
- 1 cucumber, diced
- 1 C yellow grape tomatoes, cut into halves
- 1 red pepper, diced
- 5 large ripe strawberries, sliced
- 1/2 C blueberries
- Top with your favorite ready-made poppy seed or strawberry vinaigrette dressing and 1/2 C crumbled feta cheese (if desired)

DIRECTIONS

1. Layer each item in order. Serve with the dressing and cheese, if you do dairy.

CONTRIBUTOR NOTES

Omit the cheese for a vegan recipe

This is what America looks like—all different shapes, colors and types!

Submitted by: Judith Luber-Narod

"Democrats, this is our fight. This is the only fight. This is our story, our message, our electoral strategy and our moral responsibility. To rebuild a country defined by the decency it offers every proud man, woman or child who is blessed to call this nation home. Where strength isn't measured by who you prey on, but who you protect. Where greatness isn't just a show of muscle, but of mercy. Where we understand that a

nation cannot be powerful if its people are powerless." - Congressman Joe Kennedy III.

LETTUCE MARCH FOR PEAS (V or OLV)

Serves 4

INGREDIENTS

- One large or two small romaine lettuce heads (about 4 to 5 C) torn or coarsely sliced
- 1 1/2 C fresh peas or thawed frozen peas
- 1 to 3 TB butter, olive oil or coconut oil
- 1 TB fresh tarragon or 1 tsp dried tarragon

- Salt and pepper to taste

DIRECTIONS

1. Heat oil or butter on medium heat. Add lettuce and sauté while stirring about 3 minutes.
2. Add peas and tarragon and continue sautéing and stirring an additional 5 minutes or so until the lettuce is softened and just barely starting to brown.
3. Remove from heat, add salt and pepper, and serve.

CONTRIBUTOR NOTES

This is a classic French recipe, so a more generous amount of butter is more traditional. But it tastes good with a smaller amount of olive or coconut oil so make it to your own taste. Freshly shelled spring peas are amazing in this recipe if you can get them and feel like shelling them, but frozen ones work fine. You can also experiment with the herb; consider mint or lavender or whatever you have fresh.

Submitted by: Joan Berglund

"In Boston on Saturday, counter protesters flooded the city to march for unity as well as overwhelmingly oppose what animated the [white nationalist] rally in Virginia, especially since some of that event's organizers were supposed to attend the Boston rally. In the end, counter protesters outnumbered rally-goers by as many as 800 to one." - Chas Danner, "Tens of Thousands March Against Hatred and White Supremacy in Boston, Overwhelm 'Free Speech' Rally," *NYmag.com*, August 19, 2017.

WITH OR WITHOUT YOU CORY GARDNER GAR-DEN SALAD (GF, OLV)

Serves 4 to 6

INGREDIENTS

- 1 C torn fresh mint leaves
- 1/3 C thinly sliced red onion
- One 6 oz package baby kale leaves
- 1/4 C plain Greek yogurt
- 2 TB buttermilk
- 2 tsp white wine vinegar
- 1 1/2 tsp extra-virgin olive oil
- 1/4 tsp salt
- 1/4 tsp ground black pepper
- 4 hard-boiled large eggs, quartered
- One 8 oz package of peeled, steamed, and quartered red baby beets
- 1/2 C chopped walnuts
- 1/2 C blue cheese, crumbled

DIRECTIONS

1. Combine mint, onion, and kale in large bowl.
2. Whisk together yogurt, buttermilk, vinegar, oil, salt, and pepper in separate bowl.
3. Drizzle yogurt mixture over kale, mint, and onion, and toss to coat.
4. Arrange eggs and beets over salad.
5. Sprinkle nuts and cheese over salad.

CONTRIBUTOR NOTES

This Gardner "Garden" Salad displays the colors of the Centennial State's flag: gold for abundant sunshine, white for snowcapped mountains, blue for clear Colorado skies, and red for the state's ruddy earth.

When U.S. Senator Cory Gardner refused to hold Town Halls during the February 2017 recess, Coloradans hosted a "With or Without You" meeting. Packed into a Denver middle school gym and cafeteria, constituents symbolically posed questions regarding health care, climate change, and immigration to a large cardboard cutout photo of Gardner taped to a lectern.

Submitted by: Seven Sister Resister

ANOTHER ONE BITES THE CRUST GARLIC BREAD (OLV)

Serves 6-8

INGREDIENTS

- Loaf of good, fresh Italian bread
- 1/2 stick butter
- 3 to 4 garlic cloves, sliced
- Parmesan cheese
- Mozzarella cheese shredded (1/3 package)
- Dash of paprika

DIRECTIONS

1. In small sauce pan simmer fresh garlic in butter (don't let it brown).
2. Slice bread in half along the length.
3. Pour garlic butter mixture down center of loaf.
4. Sprinkle with parmesan cheese and mozzarella cheese.
5. Bake in 350-degree oven on a baking sheet for 10-15 minutes (watch it doesn't burn).
6. Sprinkle with a dash of paprika before slicing and serving.

CONTRIBUTOR NOTES

Before I became sensitive to both garlic and gluten (ugh, I know) I used to make this bread all the time. Now I share it with you. Please enjoy it for me. Note, if you can find GF Italian bread (good luck with that) it would also be delicious, but probably not as good without the garlic though.

Submitted by: Pamela Lowell

"The Trump administration has become a bit of a revolving door since President Donald Trump took office in January. Plagued by controversy and criticism, the Trump team has struggled to craft a united front amid widespread personnel turnover that's featured high-profiled firings and swift resignations alike." - Megan Trimble, "These People Lasted Less Than 7 Months With Trump in the White House," *US-News.com*, July 31, 2017.

FLYNN'S TURKISH TATER TOSS (GF, V)

Serves 4

INGREDIENTS

- 2 to 3 lb potatoes in cut into 1 1/2 inch chunks
- 1 to 3 TB of olive oil to taste
- 1/2 to 1 tsp of ras el hanout Turkish spice mix (Trader Joe's is one brand, or buy online)
- Salt to taste (there's a fair amount of black pepper in the spice mix already)

DIRECTIONS

1. Preheat oven to 425 degrees Fahrenheit.
2. Add potatoes to your roasting pan, toss with olive oil and spices.
3. Roast, stirring every 10 minutes, until cooked through and starting to brown and crisp. This should take about 30 to 40 minutes.

CONTRIBUTOR NOTES

I like to use a mix of white, blue and sweet potatoes. It's also good with carrots and cauliflower added if you want your starchy carbs and fibrous carbs in the same dish. The full teaspoon of Ras El Hanout will have some heat since it contains chili and cayenne, so proceed at your own risk. If you are going to use the lower amount of olive oil, you may want to spray your pan with cooking spray to prevent sticking.

Submitted by: Joan Berglund

"One of the Trump administration's first decisions about the fight against the Islamic State was made by Michael Flynn weeks before he was fired—and it conformed to the wishes of Turkey, whose interests, unbeknownst to anyone in Washington, he'd been paid more than $500,000 to represent." - Vera Bergengruen, "Flynn stopped military plan Turkey opposed—after being paid as its agent," *MiamiHerald.com*, May 17, 2017.

"The facts increasingly finger the Flynn family for flimflammery." - Ron Klain, *The Lawrence O'Donnell Show*, September 13, 2017.

WHITE BEAN ARTICHOKE SALAD (GF, V)
(Not Steak with Ketchup)

INGREDIENTS

Salad

- Two 15 oz cans white cannellini beans, rinsed and drained
- 2 cans artichoke hearts, rinsed and quartered
- 1 small red onion, diced
- 2 celery stalks, thinly sliced
- One 6 oz can black olives, drained, halved
- 2 TB chopped fresh oregano

Dressing

- 1/2 cup olive oil
- 1/4 cup fresh lemon juice
- 1 clove garlic, thinly sliced (or more, to taste)
- 1/4 tsp red pepper flakes
- 1 tsp ground fennel seeds
- Kosher salt and freshly ground black pepper

DIRECTIONS

1. Make dressing by whisking all ingredients together. Let stand at least 30 minutes.
2. In a large bowl, combine artichokes, beans, onion, celery, olives, and oregano.
3. Add dressing and toss to coat.
4. Transfer to a serving bowl or platter. Serve at room temperature.

CONTRIBUTOR NOTES

Can be made 24 hours in advance. Remove from fridge 30 minutes in advance of serving.

Submitted by: Susan Jane

"Recently, the public learned that the White House kitchen staff knows to deliver their boss extra Thousand Island dressing and a double serving of ice cream while his guests get vinaigrette and a single scoop of vanilla, triggering sniggers about presidential gluttony. And since Trump so shamelessly slings stingingly personal insults tied to fitness and body type—from 'Miss Piggy' to 'fat pig' to 'Little Marco'—why resist the urge to poke his proverbial soft underbelly? We should resist, because Trump's attitudes toward healthy eating and exercise aren't a joke—they have serious consequences for the nation's health." - Natalia Mehlman Petrzela, "Why Donald Trump's diet is bad for America's health," W*ashingtonPost.com,* June 28, 2017.

HEADLINE MEALS

KELLYANNE'S MICROWAVED POACHED SESAME SALMON (GF)

Serves 2-4

INGREDIENTS

- 2 to 4 salmon filets
- 1 tsp olive oil
- 1 tsp sesame oil
- 1 tsp grated ginger
- 1/4 C fresh basil, sliced thin

DIRECTIONS

1. Place salmon filets on parchment paper. Drizzle with olive and sesame oil, grated ginger, salt and pepper and basil.
2. Fold or wrap parchment paper tightly around salmon.
3. Microwave 4-6 minutes (on cook) till salmon flakes easily.

Submitted by Nancy Skilton. Feel the Bern supporter.

"What I can say is there are many ways to surveil each other now, unfortunately. There was an article this week that talked about how you can surveil someone through their phones, through their, certainly through their television sets, any number of different ways, and microwaves that turn into cameras, etc. So we know that this is just a fact of modern life." - Kellyanne Conway, interview by Bergen Record, March 12, 2017.

"And, when the top one-tenth of 1% now owns almost as much wealth as the bottom 90%, that's not fair. It is not fair when the 20 wealthiest people in this country now own more wealth than the bottom half of the American people. So, are you guys ready for a radical idea? Together we are going to create an economy that works for all of us, not just the 1%." - Bernie Sanders, New Hampshire Democratic primary victory speech.

VEGETARIAN FAKE GROUND ROUND ... OR: IM-POTUS BEEF (GF, V)

Makes the equivalent of 2 lb of ground beef in recipes

INGREDIENTS

- 2 C textured vegetable protein crumbles (Bob's Red Mill or order online)
- 1 TB crushed garlic
- Vegetable oil
- Veggie bouillon cube (Knorr or Osem make good ones)
- 2 C liquid made up of 2 TB soy sauce and boiling water
- Extras: taco seasoning, black beans

DIRECTIONS

1. Boil hot water and measure out 2 separate cups. Add bouillon to 1 cup of water (that's half a cube of Knorr vegetarian or 1 tsp of Osem onion bouillon).

Once thoroughly dissolved, add the rest of the ingredients.

2. Measure out 2 cups of textured vegetable protein and pour the rest of the very hot liquid over it, mixing occasionally until it is entirely absorbed.

3. Once the liquid is entirely absorbed, pan fry with oil and allow to brown a little. If you want to use it for tacos, throw in a handful of black beans, taco seasoning and some water while pan frying. Voila! Taco meat.

CONTRIBUTOR NOTES

This recipe makes the equivalent of 2 lb of ground beef in recipe, and is comparable to Morningstar and Boca Crumbles. You can freeze it too. Note that the color of it will be lighter than the dark brown of meat or the dark brown of the commercial products, but won't be noticed when part of recipes like lasagna, etc.

Submitted by: Poison Paulie

"It's going to be very difficult. I don't see this president-elect as a legitimate president. I think the Russians participated in helping this man get elected, and they helped destroy the candidacy of Hillary Clinton. That's not right. That's not fair. That's not the open democratic process." - Congressman John Lewis, interview by Chuck Todd, *Meet the Press*, January 13, 2017.

THREE LITTLE CHAUVINIST PIGS

Serves 6-8

INGREDIENTS

Brine

- 3 lb boneless pork loin, butterflied (not a tenderloin—different cut of meat)
- 1/2 C sea salt
- 1/4 C maple syrup
- 4 garlic cloves
- 1 TB rosemary
- 1 bay leaf
- 1 TB whole black peppercorns

Sausage Cornbread Stuffing

- 1 TB butter
- 1/2 lb sweet Italian sausage, casings removed
- 1/2 yellow or white onion, chopped
- 2 celery stalks, chopped
- 2 garlic cloves, chopped
- 1 C chicken broth
- 1/4 to 1/2 tsp ground black pepper
- 1/2 tsp salt (if using low sodium chicken broth)
- 4 C cornbread
- 1 TB sage
- 1 TB thyme
- 1/2 TB rosemary
- 1 C dried cherries
- 2 packs uncured bacon (such as Uncured Maple Brined Bacon Vermont Smoke & Cure) (reserve 2 slices)

Cherry Reduction

- 2 slices bacon
- 1 shallot

- 1 TB balsamic vinegar
- 1/2 C red wine
- 1/2 C chicken stock
- 1/4 cherry preserves
- 1/2 tsp thyme
- Pinch nutmeg
- 1 TB butter

DIRECTIONS

Brine the pork loin (24-48 hours before serving time)

1. Add warm (not hot) water to a large, leak-proof plastic bag, 6-8 C.
2. Stir in the salt and maple syrup.
3. Add the garlic, rosemary, bay leaf, and peppercorns and pork loin.
4. Place bag in a bowl and then put in the fridge for 1-2 days.

Make the cornbread stuffing (24-48 hours before serving time)

1. Preheat the oven to 375 degrees Fahrenheit.
2. Heat oil in a butter in a large skillet over medium heat. Add sausage to the skillet and cook, breaking it up with a spatula. The sausage should be browned and cooked through, about 7 minutes. Using a slotted spoon or spatula, transfer sausage to a bowl and set aside.
3. Do not clean the pan. Add the celery and onion and cook, about 4 minutes. Add in the garlic and cook about 4 minutes longer. Then add broth, salt (if necessary), and ground pepper. Bring to boil.
4. While the broth mixture comes to a boil, add the cornbread to the sausage, breaking it up with your hands as you add it. Then add broth mixture to the bowl and stir until well-combined. Mix in rosemary, sage, thyme, and the cherries.

5. Transfer to a 9-inch casserole dish and bake until hot throughout, 25 to 30 minutes.
6. Let the stuffing come to room temperature before adding to the pork loin.

Prepare and cook the roast

1. Preheat oven to 325 degrees Fahrenheit and put aluminum foil at the bottom of a shallow pan.
2. Remove the roast from the brine and rinse. Pat dry and spread on the countertop or large cutting board. Cover the meat with plastic wrap and pound using a meat tenderizer until the meat has an even thickness of about 3/4 of an inch.
3. Spread an even layer of cornbread sausage stuffing, leaving about 1/4 inch margins at the sides of the meat. This will help keep the stuffing inside the meat roll.
4. Roll the meat into a tube shape and place inside the pan. Keep the "seam" on the underside of the roast to hold the roll in place.
5. Place the bacon over the roast. You can simply layer the slices, or create a "basketweave" pattern from slices on your cutting board, and then transfer the bacon blanket over the meat roll. Hold the bacon in place with toothpicks if necessary.
6. Cook for about 1 hour (20 minutes per pound). Meat should reach 145 degrees Fahrenheit. When the roast is almost done cooking, you can put the rest of the stuffing back in the oven to warm up.

Optional: Make the Cherry Reduction

While the roast is cooking, make your sauce.

1. Chop the reserved slices of bacon and sauté in a skillet.
2. Once cooked, remove the bacon. Add shallot, cook until translucent. Add stock, wine, thyme, and nutmeg. Cook over medium-high for 5 minutes.

3. Add the preserves and simmer 5 more minutes. Once the sauce is to your desired thickness remove from heat and stir in butter.

Finishing

1. To crisp the bacon, turn your broiler on low for about 3 minutes. Let the meat rest for 5 minutes before slicing. Serve with the warmed stuffing and the cherry reduction.

Submitted by: Maxine Rodham Ginsburg Yates

"Gloria Steinem explained why men have as much at stake in feminism as women. 'I would say that each of us has only one thing to gain from the feminist movement: Our whole humanity,' she said. 'Because gender has wrongly told us that some things are masculine and some things are feminine…which is bullshit.'" - Alanna Vagianos, "Gloria Steinem On What Men Have To Gain From Feminism," *HuffingtonPost.com*, March 6, 2015.

RECLAIMING MY TIME ROOT BEER BBQ SHREDDED PORK (GF)

Serves 6-8

INGREDIENTS

- 1 boneless 3 to 4 lb pork shoulder (butt)
- 12 to 16 oz root beer, enough to mostly cover the meat in your crock pot (feel free to eyeball it)
- One 18 oz bottle barbecue sauce of your choice—something with a little bit of peppery "bite" to it will withstand heat and prolonged cooking in a slow cooker and get sweeter as it warms up

DIRECTIONS

1. Prep your pork shoulder. Remove large pads of fat on the roast, if any. Place the roast in your regular-sized crock pot. Pour root beer over the meat.

2. Cook, covered, on low heat, 8 to 10 hours.
3. When the meat is fully cooked, remove it from the crock pot and allow it to cool slightly while you discard the liquids left over from cooking.
4. Use two forks, or other suitable implements, to shred the meat to the bite-size of your preference. Return all of the shredded meat to the cooker.
5. Pour all of the barbecue sauce over the meat, stir to incorporate, and continue to heat on the "low" setting for at least 30 more minutes.
6. Serve on buns (preferably with a sliced sweet pickle with a little spicy zing to it), on nachos, eat it with a fork, or scoop it up with tortilla chips. You do you.

Submitted by: Rachel Trousdale

"During a hearing of the House Finances Committee, Congresswoman Maxine Waters asked Treasury Secretary Steve Mnuchin why he hadn't responded to a letter she'd sent him requesting information about Trump's financial ties to Russia. He didn't answer, and instead complimented her on her service to California. When he continued to dawdle, Waters responded, 'Reclaiming my time.' She repeated the phrase, 'Reclaiming my time'...until the committee silenced Mnuchin." - Vanessa Williams, "Maxine Waters inspires a new anthem: 'Reclaiming my time,'" *WashingtonPost.com*, August 1, 2017.

LYING RYAN'S SPINELESS CHICKEN (GF)

Serves 4-6

INGREDIENTS

- One whole roasting chicken OR chicken thighs, breasts, legs, OR a combo (enough to feed your family)
- 1 onion
- 2 celery stalks
- 3 to 4 carrots (more, if you love carrots)

- About 1 level tsp of salt
- Pinch of pepper
- Pinch of garlic powder
- Ketchup—to your taste and discretion—the more, the merrier
- Couple pinches of paprika
- Pinch of sugar to cut acidic level of ketchup and of paprika (optional)

DIRECTIONS

1. Cut veggies into slightly larger than bite-sized pieces.
2. Place in Dutch oven (large pot).
3. Distribute ketchup over veggies and add spices.
4. Add 1/2 C to 1 C boiling water—you might need more to cover veggies.
5. Simmer about 20 minutes on the stove stop at medium heat.
6. Add chicken on top.
7. Continue to cook on medium to medium-low heat for about an hour (do not let it boil).
8. Then turn heat level to low and let simmer "forever" for super-soft chicken!!
9. Serve with rice or egg noodles and enjoy!

Submitted by: Justice Sandi

BREAKING: There's an inflatable chicken with Trump's hair behind the White House." - @RebeccaShabad, *Twitter.com*, August 9, 2017.

WE WON'T CHILL-I OUT TILL TRUMP'S GONE

Serves 6-8

INGREDIENTS

- 2 lb ground beef
- 1 lb sweet Italian sausage

- 1 lb bacon
- Three 15 oz cans of beans (drained)
- One 15 oz can of chili beans in sauce (don't drain)
- Two 28 oz cans of diced tomatoes with juice
- One 6 oz can of tomato paste
- 1 large yellow onion, chopped
- 3 stalks celery, chopped
- 1 green bell pepper, chopped
- 1 red bell pepper, chopped
- 2 green chili peppers, chopped
- 4 C chicken or beef stock
- 1/4 C chili powder
- 1 TB Worcestershire sauce
- 1 TB minced garlic
- 1 TB dried oregano
- 2 tsp cumin
- 2 tsp hot sauce
- 1 tsp dried basil
- 1 tsp ground black pepper
- 1 tsp cayenne
- 1 tsp paprika
- 1 tsp white sugar

DIRECTIONS

1. Pour chili beans, spicy chili beans, diced tomatoes and tomato paste into large stock pot or crock pot. Add stock. Add all spices. Stir to blend well. Set to low heat.
2. Chop all vegetables.
3. Remove casing from sausage and crumble into pan over medium-high heat. Cook until brown. Drain excess grease.
4. Cook ground beef until brown. Drain excess grease.
5. Chop bacon into bits. Cook until slightly crispy (this takes longer than cooking whole slices). Drain most of the excess grease. Save some in pan for sautéing vegetables.

6. Sauté all peppers in bacon grease until soft. Add to stock pot.
7. Sauté onions in bacon grease until soft. Add to stock pot.
8. Add chopped celery.
9. Stir to blend.
10. Simmer on low heat for 2-4 hours. You will want to cook it down until the chili is no longer watery.
11. Serve with cheddar cheese, sour cream, scallions, corn chips or your other favorite toppings!

Submitted by: S. Wright

"Six months after Women's March, Invigorated Resistance Sees Impact. Women have become more engaged in politics since Donald Trump's inauguration a new poll finds. Fifty-eight percent of women reported they had become more engaged in politics, compared with 46 percent of men." - Julia Conley, "Six Months After Women's March, Invigorated Resistance Sees Impact," *CommonDreams.org*, July 21, 2017.

LOCKER ROOM TALK-OS

Serves 4-6

INGREDIENTS

- 1 lb ground beef
- 12 hard or soft taco shells
- 2 C shredded lettuce
- 2 C shredded cheddar or Mexican blend cheese
- 2 C salsa of choice
- 1/2 C sour cream

DIRECTIONS

1. Sauté ground beef in a skillet over medium high heat until browned and no longer pink.
2. Drain beef, add 1 C of salsa and stir.

3. Simmer for an additional 2-3 minutes or until flavors combine.
4. While the beef is cooking, heat taco shells at 350 degrees Fahrenheit for 10 minutes for hard, or for 25 seconds on high on a microwave safe plate covered by a damp paper towel for soft.

Submitted by: Douglas Chicca

"When you're a star, they let you do it." - Donald Trump, Access Hollywood tape.

"Over the past 55 years I have been in many locker rooms: football, track, high school, college, racquetball, country club, golf. I have never heard in them the language used by Donald Trump." - Daniel Pellegrin, "Donald Trump, 'Locker-Room Talk' and Sexual Assault," Letter to the Editor, *NYTimes.com*, October 10, 2016.

SCARAMUCCI'S BEEF WITH THE PRESS

INGREDIENTS

- 3 lb beef chuck roast
- 2 TB minced garlic
- 8 oz sliced pepperoncini with brine
- 1 can low sodium beef broth
- Provolone cheese slices
- Focaccia bread or sub rolls

DIRECTIONS

1. Place chuck roast in the bottom of a 5.5 or 6 qt crockpot.
2. Cover with beef broth, pepperoncini with brine and minced garlic.
3. Cook on low for 8 hours.
4. Shred beef with a fork, mixing in pepperoncini.

5. Place one piece of focaccia bread (or half of a split sub roll) in a grill pan or on a panini press.
6. Top with 2 slices of provolone cheese and place other piece of bread on top.
7. If using the panini press, press the sandwich following your appliance directions.
8. If using a grill pan, use a cookie sheet or a flat skillet weighted down with a canned good to "press" the sandwich.

Submitted by: Ruth Chicca

"Anthony Scaramucci called me to unload about White House leakers Reince Priebus and Steve Bannon. He started by threatening to fire the entire White House communications staff. It escalated from there." - Ryan Lizza, "Anthony Scaramucci Called Me to Unload About White House Leakers, Reince Priebus, and Steve Bannon," *NewYorker.com*, July 27, 2017.

BAD HOMBRE CHILI (GF)

Serves 6-8

INGREDIENTS

- 1 big onion
- 1 big green bell pepper
- 1 lb or so boneless skinless chicken thighs
- 1 lb or so boneless skinless chicken breast
- 2 to 4 canned chipotles in adobo sauce, to taste, finely chopped
- A little chopped garlic
- 1 tsp cumin
- 1 can of beer
- 3 cans of beans; use 3 different color beans
- One 20 oz can of diced tomato. (You can also use two 14 oz cans, but it will be a little too tomatoey, but

that's not the end of the world. You can also use diced tomato with green chilies, that's a nice touch.)
- 1 bag of frozen corn.
- Salt and pepper to taste.
- Chopped cilantro (optional, because some of you Philistines don't like cilantro)

DIRECTIONS

1. In a big saucepan, put a little cooking oil, chop that onion and pepper, and throw it in the pan over a high heat. Throw the thighs in, slice the breasts across the grain about 3 to 4 slices out of each breast, toss in and stir. Add chipotle.
2. Toss the garlic in. Let it sweat down a little while stirring. Let it sweat a little longer.
3. Mmmm...is it almost burning? Oops. Throw 1/2 the can of beer in and lower the temp to medium-high. Drink the other 1/2 beer unless it's a cheap beer, then give it to the dog or throw it in the sink.
4. Put the tomatoes in and stir it around. Open the cans of beans while letting the mix reduce over medium-high heat. Rinse the beans. Or there may be gas. A lot. Do everyone a favor and rinse them. There'll still be gas. But less. Less is good.
5. Throw the beans in, lower heat to low-medium. Let it reduce more, maybe 20-30 minutes. Stir once in a while, so it don't burn or stick, ya nitwit.
6. Add 1/2 of the corn unless you're a huge fan of corn, stir, let it cook a little longer, reduce more if needed. If it looks really wet, increase heat and stir more often. Add your salt and pepper and cilantro if using.
7. There! Done! It's awesome. It will be best tomorrow.

CONTRIBUTOR NOTES

You can use cheap beer, or good beer, whatever you use will give it a slightly different tone: domestic pilsner will sweeten it up, as will porter or stout. IPA will give it a little bitterness which is OK. Just don't use like a Hefeweizen, summer wheat, or Belgian wit.

Use 3 different color beans. It will make it pretty. Can you use 3 cans of black beans or 3 cans of pinto beans? Yes, of course you can. But it won't be as pretty.

Variation: Add about 2 C of sweet potato or butternut squash or any sweet firm squash, in 1/2 inch cubes. It sounds weird, but it's really good. Trust me, add the sweet potatoes. Chipotle and sweet potatoes go together like peanut butter and bacon. Throw 'em in shortly after the beans. When they're done, the dish is done.

Submitted by: Richard Paige

"Well, now we know Trump's Spanish vocabulary is all of 2 words: 'hombre' and 'taco'. I'd gladly teach him a few more choice words." - @ananavarro, *Twitter.com*, October 19, 2016.

I'M STILL WITH HER LASAGNA

INGREDIENTS

- Your favorite lasagna recipe
- Small pepperoni circle slices (bag)

DIRECTIONS

1. Prepare lasagna.
2. On top of lasagna place pepperoni in I'm With Her design (H with arrow pointing right).

Submitted by: Pamela Lowell

"Final Popular Vote Total Shows Hillary Clinton Won Almost 3 Million More Ballots than Donald Trump. It's by far the largest margin of victory in the popular vote for a candidate who did not win the election." - Nick Wing, *Huffingtonpost.com,* December 20, 2016.

When a candidate who wins the popular vote does not take office, when a loser is instead installed in the White House, that is an issue. And it raises questions that must be addressed." - John Nichols, "Hillary Clinton's Popular-Vote Victory Is Unprecedented—and Still Growing," *TheNation.com*, November 16, 2016.

"So, yes, I'm still with her! Why wouldn't I be? She should have been our 45th President and, if she was, you can bet that we wouldn't be spending all of our time and energy fighting against Muslim bans and the rollback of transgender rights in the military, begging to save the Affordable Care Act and programs like DACA, and having an actual conversation about whether there is more than one side to blame at a violent neo-Nazi rally." - Jennifer Rand, "Defending Hillary: Damn Right I'm 'Still With Her' And Here's Why," *HuffingtonPost.com*, September 7, 2017.

PRESIDENTIAL EGGPLANT PARDON-ME-GIANA (OLV)

Serves 9-12

INGREDIENTS

- 2 medium eggplants (I prefer thin ones)
- 2 C seasoned breadcrumbs
- 3 large eggs
- 1 jar pasta sauce (I use Prego Spinach Florentine)
- 1/2 TB milk
- Canola oil
- 1 large bag shredded mozzarella cheese
- 1 small container of ricotta

DIRECTIONS

Prep

1. Make egg wash by whisking eggs and milk.
2. Pour 1 C of breadcrumbs on a plate. You will add more later as needed.

3. Cut eggplant into 1/8 to 1/4 inch thick slices.
4. Pour enough canola oil into frying pan so it is about 1/4 inch deep. Turn on medium heat.

Cooking

1. Dip eggplant slices into egg wash and then into breadcrumbs, coating evenly.
2. Once oil is heated, drop eggplant in. They should start sizzling immediately; otherwise oil is not hot enough. I usually have the oil on medium-low heat (3-4). Adjust as needed.
3. Cook eggplant until slightly brown, about 3-4 minutes on each side. A fork should go through easily. Do not overcook.
4. Transfer eggplant to a plate lined with paper towels to drain oil.
5. Preheat oven to 350.

Assembly

1. Coat the bottom of a 9x13 baking dish with a thin layer of sauce.
2. Place a layer of the cooked eggplant down, covering the bottom.
3. Place a spoonful of sauce on each slice of eggplant and use back of spoon to spread it. Each should be lightly covered with sauce.
4. Put a dollop of ricotta on top of each eggplant slice.
5. Repeat steps 2-4 until you have about 4-5 layers, depending on pan depth.
6. Cover generously with shredded mozzarella cheese.
7. Bake for 35-45 minutes, or until cheese is bubbly and starts to brown.

Submitted by: Sharon and Kristin Winsett

"Trump has consulted his legal advisers about the possibility of pre-emptively pardoning his associates—and possibly even himself—to undermine the Justice Department's Russia investigation, The Washington Post reported Thursday

night." - Charlie Savage, "Can Trump Pardon Himself? Explaining Presidential Clemency Powers," *NewYork-Times.com*, July 21, 2017.

2016 VOTERS WERE BROCCOLI ROBBED PASTA DISH

Serves 4 to 6

INGREDIENTS

- 2 bunches broccoli rabe, trim off tough stem ends
- 1 lb orecchiette pasta
- 3 TB olive oil
- 1 lb Italian sausage with casings removed (Italian turkey sausage also works great)
- 3 or more garlic cloves minced
- Pinch dried crushed red pepper flakes
- 1/4 C freshly grated Parmesan cheese

DIRECTIONS

1. Cook the broccoli rabe in large pot of boiling salted water until crisp tender (1-2 minutes). Transfer (lift out with tongs or slotted spoon) the broccoli rabe to a large bowl of ice water to cool, save the cooking water and bring back to a boil.
2. Heat oil in large skillet over medium heat, add the sausage and cook breaking it up into smaller pieces with a spoon until browned and juices form (about 12-15 minutes).
3. Add the garlic and red pepper flakes and sauté until fragrant (about 2 minutes).
4. Meanwhile, when the reserved cooking water is boiling add the pasta and cook until al dente, tender but still firm to the bite, stirring occasionally.
5. Strain the broccoli rabe and add it to the pan with the sausage mixture and toss to coat with the juices. Add the pasta to the skillet, stir in the parmesan and serve immediately. Put extra Parmesan on table to sprinkle on pasta. Enjoy!

CONTRIBUTOR NOTES

I always use orecchiette shaped pasta, it works great to hold the sausage pieces, but any shaped pasta works, like shells, fusilli and cavatappi.

Submitted by: Karen Letendre

"It's becoming pretty evident that Russia was actively intending and acting to subvert our principal exercise in democracy by doing precisely what the original intent of Watergate was: stealing secrets from the Democratic Party and using them to undermine the party's campaign. Mission accomplished this time." - Tom Toles, "The 2016 election was stolen. Got a nicer way to say that?" Opinions, *WashingtonPost.com*, December 16, 2016.

HE AIN'T GOT A NOODLE SAVORY STRUDEL (OLV)

Serves 6-8

INGREDIENTS

- 1/2 onion
- 1 red pepper
- 1 white mushroom
- 1 sheet of puff pastry (like Wewalka)
- 1 C of ricotta or small curd cottage cheese
- 1/2 C shredded cheddar
- 1/2 C mozzarella
- 1 TB grated Parmesan
- 1 raw egg beaten
- Vegetable oil
- Optional: pasta sauce for dipping, olive or other veggie add-ins

DIRECTIONS

1. Preheat the oven to 400 degrees Fahrenheit. Stir fry sliced onions and red pepper, adding mushroom half way through cooking. Sauté until soft.
2. Mix together the ricotta/cottage cheese, cheddar, mozzarella and Parmesan. Add half the beaten egg and mix well. I like to microwave for 30 seconds and pour out any excess liquid.
3. Lay out a cookie sheet and roll out the puff pastry sheet leaving the parchment paper underneath the dough sheet, lying directly on the pan.
4. Laying the pan lengthwise, spread the vegetable mixture on one half of the dough. Spoon the cheese mixture on top and spread it evenly.
5. Now fold over the dough so that you make a pocket that looks like a long calzone. Use a fork to press little marks on the three open sides and seal the pocket.

6. Finally, brush the rest of the beaten egg onto the exposed side of the pocket. This will help make a golden glaze.
7. Cook for about 20 minutes, until the pastry has risen and is a pleasing golden color. If necessary, rotate the pan so that all sides are evenly browned.

CONTRIBUTOR NOTES

You can change up the vegetables, add black olive, etc. but stir-fried onions always add to the flavor.

September 2017: A week after author Stephen King bans Trump from seeing his new movie, Trump supporters angrily announce a loud boycott. The film *It* then proceeds to smash box office records, earning a whopping $123 million during its opening weekend, proving once and for all that Americans would rather watch a fictional evil clown over an actual one.

Submitted by: Poison Paulie

"Trump proposes 'IQ tests' faceoff with Secretary of State Rex Tillerson after the nation's top diplomat reportedly called the president a 'moron' and disparaged his grasp of foreign policy." - Philip Rucker, *WashingtonPost.com,* October 10, 2017.

PATRIOT PANCAKES (OLV)

Serves 4

INGREDIENTS

- 1 1/2 C all-purpose flour
- 3 1/2 tsp baking powder
- 1 tsp salt
- 1 TB sugar
- 1 tsp cinnamon
- 1 tsp nutmeg
- 1 1/4 C milk
- 1/2 tsp vanilla
- 1 egg
- 3 TB unsalted, melted butter
- 1 C blueberries
- 1 C strawberries
- Whipped cream

DIRECTIONS

1. In a large bowl, sift together all dry ingredients. Set aside.
2. In a separate bowl, beat one egg, add in melted butter, vanilla and milk, beat lightly.
3. Add wet ingredients to dry ingredients.
4. Heat griddle over medium heat.
5. Pour or scoop (one ice cream scoop size) batter onto the griddle. Drop in a few blueberries per pancake. Brown on both sides.
6. Serve warm and top with fresh strawberries and blueberries. Whipped cream optional!

Submitted by: Liberty Beth

"Patriotism means to stand by the country. It does not mean to stand by the president or any other public official, save exactly to the degree in which he himself stands by the country. In either event, it is unpatriotic not to tell the truth,

whether about the president or anyone else." - Theodore Roosevelt

"Donald Trump, you are asking Americans to trust you with our future. Let me ask you: Have you even read the U.S. Constitution? I will gladly lend you my copy. In this document, look for the words 'liberty' and 'equal protection of law.' Have you ever been to Arlington Cemetery? Go look at the graves of the brave patriots who died defending America -- you will see all faiths, genders and ethnicities." - Khizr Khan, father of U.S. Army Captain Humayun Khan killed in Iraq in 2004, to the Democratic National Convention in Philadelphia, July 28, 2016.

GOP MUMBO GUMBO

Serves 4-6

INGREDIENTS

- 1/4 C all-purpose flour
- 1 TB vegetable oil
- 1 C onion, chopped
- 1 C green bell pepper, chopped
- 3 garlic cloves, chopped
- 1 tsp dried thyme
- 1 bay leaf
- 3 low-fat Italian turkey sausages (about 10 oz), casings removed
- One 28 oz can diced tomatoes in juice
- 1 C canned low-salt chicken broth or vegetable broth
- 2 tsp Creole or Cajun seasoning
- 12 uncooked large shrimp, peeled, deveined
- 2 cans lump crabmeat

DIRECTIONS

1. Sprinkle flour over bottom of heavy large pot. Stir flour constantly over medium-low heat until flour

turns golden brown (do not allow to burn), about 15 minutes. Pour browned flour into bowl.

2. Heat oil in same pot over medium heat. Add onion and bell pepper and sauté until tender, about 7 minutes. Add garlic, thyme and bay leaf; stir 1 minute. Add sausages and sauté until brown, breaking up with back of spoon, about 5 minutes, then add browned flour. Add tomatoes with juices, broth and Creole seasoning. Bring to boil.

3. Reduce heat, cover and simmer 20 minutes to blend flavors, stirring frequently.

4. Add shrimp and crabmeat to pot and simmer just until seafood is opaque in center, about 5 minutes. Discard bay leaf. Season with salt and pepper and serve.

Submitted by: Jamila Lewis Greene

"The GOP is trapped in its own lies on almost every substantive policy. Healthcare isn't the only issue on which lies are coming back to bite the liars. The same story is playing out on other issues—in fact, on almost every substantive policy issue the U.S. faces." - Paul Krugman, "Trapped by Their Own Lies," Opinion, *SeattleTimes.com,* September 25, 2017.

CHINA TRIED FRIED RICE (V)

Serves 3-4 as a main dish, 6-8 as a side

INGREDIENTS

Vegan "egg"

- 1/2 12 oz pack of soft tofu
- 1 tsp sriracha (use a brand with evaporated cane juice instead of sugar if you are a strict vegan)
- 1/2 tsp salt
- 1 TB soy sauce
- 1 TB toasted sesame oil
- 1 tsp turmeric

Rice

- 4 C cooked rice (I use brown)
- 2 to 3 carrots, chopped
- 1 medium onion, chopped
- 1 1/2 C snow peas, cut into bite-size pieces
- Peanut oil

DIRECTIONS

1. Put all the ingredients for the sauce in a blender, liquids first. You may need to stop and stir a couple of times, but it should blend up easily enough.
2. Heat the peanut oil in a pan or wok on medium-high heat.
3. Add the onions and carrots, cook, stirring constantly, for about 5-7 minutes depending on how soft you want them.
4. Add the rice. Stir and separate any clumps of rice so that the all grains get coated with oil.
5. When the rice is warm, add the peas and cook for about 3 minutes and then add the sauce. Stir it about thoroughly so that it coats all the grains of rice and let it heat thoroughly and absorb in some.

Submitted by: Joan Berglund

"While I greatly appreciate the efforts of President Xi & China to help with North Korea, it has not worked out. At least I know China tried!" - @realDonaldTrump, *Twitter.com,* June 20, 2017.

FAKE NEWDLES SQUASH ALFREDO (GF, V)

Serves 4

INGREDIENTS

Cashew cream sauce

- 2 C raw cashews
- 1 1/4 C miso ginger broth (Trader Joe's is one brand)
- Salt and pepper to taste (miso broth may already be salty enough for some people)

Newdles

- 4 medium-sized summer squash or zucchini
- 2 C cherry or grape tomatoes, halved if they are larger
- 1 TB Thai basil, sliced thin

DIRECTIONS

Sauce

1. Soak the cashews in two cups of water for at least two hours.
2. Drain the soaking liquid and process the cashews with the miso broth in a blender or food processor until smooth and creamy.

Newdles

1. Cut whole squashes into sections of about 2 inches. The size of the sections will determine the length of your zoodles. Process each section on the B blade if you have a spiralizer that has multiple blades. Refer to the instructions for your device for more details.
2. Warm all the ingredients except the basil until everything is heated through and the newdles and tomatoes are softened.
3. Remove from heat and stir in the basil.

CONTRIBUTOR NOTES

This can also be a raw dish. Use your favorite raw food diet-approved broth instead of miso broth for the cream sauce and then just mix the sauce with the prepared vegetables and serve cold or room temperature.

You can probably muddle through with a vegetable peeler, but this is easier with a spiralizer. They are readily available online for a modest amount of money—less than $20 for a counter top model with multiple blades one and less than $15 for a hand held one. They provide endless entertainment for the easily amused. You'll have some vegetable waste on the ends to save for another use (I puree them up for the dog; they can also be used for broth).

Submitted by: Joan Berglund

"'It doesn't bother me at all, but I like real news, not fake news,' Trump said, pointing at [CNN's Jim] Acosta. 'You're fake news.' 'Haven't you spread a lot of fake news yourself, sir?' Acosta shot back. Trump ignored the question and exited the room.

'The president said we just had a press conference. We did not. That's fake news,' Acosta said." - Brandon Carter, "CNN reporter to Trump: 'Haven't you spread a lot of fake news yourself?'" *TheHill.com,* August 14, 2017.

"The reason POTUS wants a fake new contest among networks is he knows he would win so in addition to the other

marvelous policy accomplishments he's racked up in his first term he could also declare himself the highest rated network." - @Merrillmarkoe, *Twitter.com*, November 27, 2017.

ROCKET MAN RIBS

Needs serving size -4-6

INGREDIENTS

- 1 medium onion, thinly sliced vertically
- 8 large cloves garlic, sliced
- 2 TB ginger, minced
- 2 C beef broth
- 1/2 C soy sauce, tamari or coconut aminos
- 1/4 C brown sugar or coconut sugar
- 2 TB unseasoned rice vinegar
- 2 TB chile paste
- 1 TB dark (toasted) sesame oil

- 2 TB plus 1 tsp vegetable oil
- Salt and black pepper
- 4 long-cut bone-in beef short ribs (2 1/2 to 3 lb), trimmed of excess fat
- 2 TB cornstarch
- 2 bunches scallions, root ends trimmed
- 2 TB toasted sesame seeds
- Kimchi
- Shredded carrots
- Cooked brown rice

DIRECTIONS

1. Combine first 9 ingredients in a slow cooker. Set slow cooker to high to preheat.
2. Heat 2 TB oil in a large skillet or sauté pan over medium-high heat. Generously season beef short ribs with salt and black pepper. Add short ribs to pan, reduce heat to medium and brown well on all sides, approximately 2-3 minutes per side.
3. Transfer ribs, meat side down, to slow cooker. Cover and cook on high for 4-6 hours or until very tender.
4. Combine cornstarch with approximately 4 TB of the cooking liquid in a small bowl and stir until smooth. Pour cornstarch mixture into slow cooker, stir to blend and cook uncovered on high for approximately 20 minutes. Turn slow cooker off and let stand 10 minutes. (Sauce will thicken more upon standing).
5. Heat remaining 1 tsp oil in a skillet or sauté pan over medium-high. Cook scallions, 2-3 minutes or until slightly softened and browned.
6. Serve short ribs with scallions, kimchi, cooked brown rice and shredded carrots.

CONTRIBUTOR NOTES

Submitted by: Jamila Lewis Greene

"'Rocket Man is on a suicide mission for himself,' President Trump told world leaders at the United Nations on Tuesday,

referring to the leader of nuclear-armed North Korea by using an epithet the president had introduced two days earlier, on Twitter, as usual." - Avi Selk, "'Rocket Man' enters Trump's U.N. speech—and the president's universe of belittling nicknames," *WashingtonPost.com*, September 19, 2017.

"North Korean leader Kim Jong Un called President Donald Trump a 'dotard' in response to Trump's speech at the United Nations General Assembly...According to Merriam-Webster, a dotard describes a person who is in a state of 'senile decay marked by decline of mental poise and alertness.'" - Mahita Gajanan, "Kim Jong Un Called President Trump a 'Dotard.' What Does That Mean?" *Time.com*, September 21, 2017.

IF IT TROTTS LIKE A CHICKEN AND TALKS LIKE A CHICKEN

INGREDIENTS

- One 8 oz package of thin rice noodles
- 2 TB sesame oil
- 1 TB olive oil
- 1 small watermelon
- 1 handful of radishes
- 4 oz of fresh mint leaves
- 4 oz of fresh cilantro leaves and stalks
- 1 TB of Chinese five spice
- 2 TB of soy sauce
- 1 TB of fish sauce
- 1-inch piece of fresh ginger
- 2 green onions
- 2 limes
- 1 unpeeled clove of garlic
- 8 skinless, boneless chicken thighs
- 2 heads of Boston lettuce
- Salt and pepper to season the chicken

DIRECTIONS

1. Toss chicken thighs with salt, pepper, and five spice in a sturdy, sealable plastic bag or large, folded piece of grease-proof paper. Flatten the chicken to a half-inch thickness with a rolling pin.
2. Fry the chicken in a large frying pan with 1 TB of olive oil until lightly charred and cooked through.
3. Boil the rice noodles according to directions on package. Once fully boiled, drain the noodles and toss them on a large serving platter with 1 TB of sesame oil.
4. Move half of the noodles to a medium frying pan, tossing them over heat until they become crunchy. Set the crunchy noodles aside.
5. Remove the watermelon rind and cut the melon into chunks. Add the chunks to the serving platter with the noodles.
6. Cut the Boston lettuce heads into small wedges and add to the serving platter.
7. Slice the radishes into small bites and add to the serving platter.
8. Finely slice the fresh mint leaves and cilantro leaves combine them with the ingredients on the serving platter.
9. Peel the fresh ginger and cut into small pieces.
10. Juice the two limes, reserving the lime juice.
11. Crush the clove of garlic.
12. In a blender, puree the cilantro stalks, the spring onions, the soy sauce, the fish sauce, the sliced ginger, 1 TB of sesame oil, the lime juice, and the crushed garlic clove. Add a TB of water, as needed, to help all ingredients blend until smooth.
13. Pour the dressing from the blender onto the serving platter and toss until the salad ingredients are well coated.
14. Slice the chicken thighs and add them to the salad mixture on the serving platter.
15. Break the crispy noodles over the top of the salad on the serving platter.

CONTRIBUTOR NOTES

Low-sodium soy sauce can be used instead of regular soy sauce. Add thinly-sliced fresh red chili pepper to the salad mixture for extra heat.

Congressman Dave Trott (R-MI) declined an invitation to attend a local town hall in suburban Detroit during the 2017 midwinter congressional recess. His constituents conducted a forum anyway, with a live chicken standing in for the man "too chicken" to face blowback on Republican efforts to repeal the Affordable Care Act.

A photo of the live chicken at the podium, tweeted by @IndivisibleMich, can be seen at https://patch.com/michigan/novi/congressman-david-trott-no-show-chicken-stands. Photos of "Chicken Trott" constituents (including one in full chicken costume) protesting outside the Congressman's home office in Troy, MI can be seen at http://www.freep.com/story/news/local/michigan/2017/02/22/representative-dave-trott-constituents/98243384/.

Submitted by: Seven Sister Resister

PASTA PUTIN-ESCA (OLV or V)

Serves 4-6

INGREDIENTS

- 8 to 10 sun-dried tomatoes sliced very thin lengthwise. Packed in oil or dry both work well.
- 3 to 4 cloves of garlic, minced
- 2 TB capers, drained
- 12 Kalamata black olives, pitted and roughly chopped
- 1 can of crushed tomatoes
- Red pepper flakes, a pinch, more if you really like extra heat.
- Olive oil
- 1 lb box of spaghetti or other long pasta

- Grated or shaved Parmesan (optional)

DIRECTIONS

1. Boil water for pasta.
2. While water is heating, place a saucepan on medium heat with a TB of olive oil. When oil is hot put sun-dried tomatoes in with red pepper flakes. Allow it to sizzle a little. Then add garlic and cook for 1 minute stirring. Add capers and olives and let cook 1 more minute. Then add can of tomatoes, undrained. Turn heat low and let simmer while you cook spaghetti.
3. Add spaghetti to boiling water and cook as directed on package. Drain and add to the saucepan with sauce. Remove from heat and toss together.
4. Serve in low bowls with a sprinkle of Parmesan, if using.

CONTRIBUTOR NOTES

Replacing sun-dried tomatoes in a classic puttanesca to make it vegan (if you skip the cheese) or vegetarian. Good hearty, warming meal for nights in the Kremlin, or the frozen heart of 45.

Submitted by: Nicole Rose

"When asked about the alleged poisoning of a vocal critic of Vladimir Putin, Sen. John McCain called Putin 'a murderer and a thug.'" - "McCain: Putin is a murderer and thug," *CNN.com*, February 9, 2017, http://www.cnn.com/videos/politics/2017/02/09/john-mccain-vladimir-putin-murderer-thug-comments-ath.cnn.

MOOCHIN' MNUCHINS' MEAL IN A MOLD

Serves 4

INGREDIENTS

- Two 6 oz cans or one 11 oz can of boneless, skinless wild-caught salmon, NOT drained
- 3 eggs
- 1/2 C anything crumbs (crumb any leftover crackers or chips you need to use up in a blender or food processor)
- 1 TB Dijon mustard
- 1 TB lemon juice
- 2 TB chopped parsley
- 2/3 C peas, fresh or thawed frozen
- 2/3 lb small potatoes (I like a mix of white, blue and sweet)
- One small or 1/2 medium onion
- 2 TB olive oil
- Cooking spray or oil for mold or pan
- Salt and pepper to taste

DIRECTIONS

1. Preheat the oven to 400 degrees Fahrenheit.
2. In a large bowl, flake the salmon with its liquid and then add in the eggs, mustard, lemon juice, parsley, peas, salt and pepper. Mix well.
3. Pour into a greased fish mold or loaf pan (it will be too loose to mold on a sheet pan).
4. Process the potatoes and onions into thin slices in a food processor. Put them into a medium bowl and drizzle with olive oil, salt and pepper. Mix thoroughly to coat.
5. Spread them in a thin layer or two over the top of your mold.
6. Bake about 40 minutes until the potatoes are soft and starting to brown.

7. If using a fish mold, put a serving platter on top of the mold and carefully invert to demold. Garnish with some olive slices for eyes.

CONTRIBUTOR NOTES

Even with wild-caught salmon and organic/certified humane eggs, this is a thrifty protein dish. Which we'll need after the Mnuchins finish spending all our money.

Submitted by: Joan Berglund

"Adorable! Do you think the U.S. govt paid for our honeymoon or personal travel?! Lololol." @LouiseLinton, *Instagram.com,* August 21, 2017.

"Treasury Secretary Steve Mnuchin took flights on military-owned aircraft costing taxpayers in excess of $800,000, a new report from the department's inspector general found.... Mnuchin has made nine requests to fly on military aircraft since taking office in February, including the withdrawn request to use a military jet for his European honeymoon." - Gabrielle Levy, "Mnuchin's Seven Military Flights Cost Taxpayers $800,000," *USNews.com,* October 6, 2017.

THE SCARAMUCCI SANDWICH

AKA "the sandmooch"

INGREDIENTS

- 2 slices white bread
- Mayonnaise
- 3 slices baloney
- 2 slices Swiss cheese

DIRECTIONS

1. Slap mayo on the bread, stack that baloney and cheese on there, and go to town.

CONTRIBUTOR NOTES

It's cheesy and full of boloney. Does not keep more than 11 days.

Submitted by: Joyce Johns and Kate Raftery

"You blazed across our skies like a comet, but you flew too close to the sun, dear Mooch." - @chrislhayes, *Twitter.com*, July 31, 2017.

GENERAL FLYNN'S CHICKEN

Serves 4

INGREDIENTS

- 1 1/2 lb chicken, skinned and boned
- 1 egg
- 1 C flour
- 1/4 pound bamboo shoots
- 1 green pepper
- 1 red pepper
- 1/4 C water
- 1 TB dark soy sauce
- 1 TB cornstarch
- Vegetable oil (for deep frying)
- 2 to 3 TB vegetable oil (in addition to the above)
- 2 cloves garlic, minced
- 1 tsp fresh ginger root, shredded
- Up to 5 black peppercorns
- 1 TB white vinegar
- 1 TB Chinese cooking wine
- 1 tsp Chinese chili sauce
- 1 TB sugar

DIRECTIONS

1. Cut the chicken into 3/4 inch cubes. In a bowl, beat the egg. Dip the chicken pieces into the egg and then dip them to coat in the flour. Set aside.

2. Cut the bamboo shoots into 1/2 inch cubes. Seed the green and red peppers and cut them into small cubes. Set aside.
3. In a small bowl, combine the water, soy sauce and cornstarch. Set aside.
4. In a wok or deep-sided, heavy-bottomed sauce pan, heat enough vegetable oil to deep fry the chicken. Deep fry the chicken until golden brown, about 10 minutes. Remove from oil and drain on paper towel.
5. Deep fry the peppers 10 seconds and remove.
6. Heat 2 to 3 TB of oil in the wok. Add chicken, peppers, garlic and ginger. Then add the remaining ingredients including the bamboo shoots but not the water-soy-cornstarch mixture and cook 2-3 minutes.
7. Add the water-soy-cornstarch mixture and simmer until sauce thickens.
8. Transfer to warmed dish and serve.

CONTRIBUTOR NOTES

General Flynn's Chicken bears a striking resemblance to General Tso's Chicken. General Tso was a well-respected 19th statesman and military leader. General Flynn is a 21st century military leader who was too chicken to admit to meeting with Russian Ambassador, Sergey Kislyak, before accepting the role of National Security Advisor.

Submitted by: Marlene Cook

CRAB CAKES FOR SMALL HANDS

INGREDIENTS

- 1 lb lump crabmeat
- 1 large egg
- 1 1/2 tsp Dijon mustard
- 1 tsp lemon juice
- 1/2 tsp Worcestershire sauce
- Kosher salt
- 1 1/4 C bread crumbs panko

- 1 TB flat leaf parsley
- 2 TB unsalted butter
- 1 TB olive oil
- 2 tsp seafood seasoning mix (Old Bay is one brand)
- 2 scallions, thinly sliced
- 1/2 C red bell pepper, finely chopped
- 2 TB nonfat milk
- Freshly ground black pepper

DIRECTIONS

1. Heat 2 TB olive oil in skillet over medium-high heat. Cook scallions and bell pepper until soft.
2. Mix 1/2 cup bread crumbs, egg, and milk in a small bowl.
3. In a medium bowl, whisk Worcestershire sauce, mustard, lemon juice, seasoning mix. Fold in bread crumbs, crabmeat, scallions, peppers, some salt and pepper.
4. Shape into 8 cakes with your dainty small hands, and refrigerate for 30 minutes.
5. Coat crab cakes with remaining breadcrumbs.
6. Heat oil over medium-high heat in clean skillet. Place crab cakes in pan and cook 3-4 minute to brown. Flip and cook 3 minutes.
7. Remove and place on paper towels. Serve warm with aioli.

CONTRIBUTOR NOTES

Triple the recipe for incredible results.

Submitted by: Susan Jane

"How did the most sensitive part of Donald Trump's anatomy become a talking point in the presidential election? Blame Graydon Carter. Nearly thirty years ago, when he was the co-editor of Spy magazine, Carter called Trump a 'short-fingered vulgarian.' According to Carter, Trump has never forgotten the insult." - Brian Stelter, "The joke about

Donald Trump's hands goes back nearly 30 years," *CNN.com*, March 4, 2016.

ORANGE A LAME DUCK (CHICKEN)

INGREDIENTS

- 1 to 2 lb chicken cut into chunks, seasoned with salt and pepper
- 2 C cooked brown or white rice

Duck sauce

- 1 jar of apricot preserves
- 2 TB rice vinegar
- 1/2 tsp ground ginger
- 1 tsp brown sugar
- Garlic to taste
- Salt to taste
- Crushed red pepper flakes to taste
- Fresh pineapple cut into chunks

DIRECTIONS

(Day before or morning of)

Duck sauce:

1. Add all ingredients to a small pot. Bring to a boil and simmer on medium for 5 minutes.
2. Let cool and refrigerate for 12-24 hours.

Grilled chicken

1. Grill chicken and set aside, or grill with the pineapple.

Grilled pineapple:

1. Cut pineapple cut into chunks. Lightly coat with canola oil. Dredge in brown sugar and salt to taste.

2. Grill on low until nice and caramelized. Flip periodically, about 30 minutes. Pineapple will have charred marks in addition to being a deep brown.
3. Serve chicken pineapple, and warmed duck sauce over a bed of cooked white or brown rice.

CONTRIBUTOR NOTES

You can add other grilled vegetables such as onions, peppers, etc.

Submitted by: Kristin Olliney-Apruzzese

"Donald Trump is a lame-duck president. Just seven months into his presidency, Trump appears to have achieved a status usually reserved for the final months of a term...The president did always brag that he was a fast learner." - David A. Graham, "Donald Trump Is a Lame-Duck President," *TheAtlantic.com*, August 17, 2017.

STEAK TIPS DONE RIGHT (WITHOUT KETCHUP)

Serves 4

INGREDIENTS

- 2 lb sirloin steak tips
- 2 C bottled Teriyaki sauce
- 4 TB minced garlic

DIRECTIONS

1. Place steak tips in a gallon zip lock bag.
2. Pour Teriyaki sauce over steak.
3. Add garlic.
4. Zip bag closed, massage steak until coated in sauce and garlic.
5. Refrigerate overnight, or at least 4 hours to marinate.

6. Grill at 325-350 degrees Fahrenheit until desired internal temperature.

CONTRIBUTOR NOTES

Medium Rare: Grill 8 minutes per side or to 140 degrees Fahrenheit internal temperature. Medium: Grill 10 minutes per side or to 155 degrees Fahrenheit internal temperature.

Submitted by: Justin Chicca

"What asshole goes to dinner at one of the nation capital's most acclaimed steakhouses, orders a 30-day dry aged New York strip, then asks the chef to cook it well done? And if that's not enough, eats it with ketchup like a 5-year-old? We'll give you one guess." - Kevin Pang, "President Trump orders his steak well done with ketchup," *AVClub.com*, February 26, 2017.

SHE PERSISTED PASTA SAUCE FOR A CROWD (V)

("Gravy" for approximately 3 pounds of pasta)

INGREDIENTS

- 5 to 6 cans of tomatoes (28 oz size) (combination of: whole, crushed or pureed)
- 1 TB parsley (fresh or dried)
- 1 TB sugar or evaporated cane juice
- 1/2 C basil, fresh, chopped (or 1/4 C dried)
- 1 tsp. salt
- 2 tsp. black pepper
- 2 to 3 cloves garlic
- 3 TB oil

DIRECTIONS

1. Open the cans of tomatoes.
2. Measure into a small bowl the parsley, sugar, basil, salt and black pepper.
3. Peel and mince the garlic.
4. Measure oil into large pot.
5. Sauté the garlic in oil on low heat for 2-3 minutes, stirring constantly. Do not let the garlic get brown.
6. Stir in all the cans of tomatoes.
7. Stir in bowl of spices/herbs.
8. Simmer 15-20 minutes, stirring occasionally - keep cover on pot when not stirring. Test taste (adjust spices/herbs to taste).
9. Add cooked meatballs or sausage, if desired. Simmer another 30 minutes.

CONTRIBUTOR NOTES

This is my Italian-American mother's recipe. As a home economics teacher, each year she made this dish with her students. She was an inspiring and empowering educator who especially advocated and cared for her more disenfranchised students. In college, she and my dad protested the Vietnam War and advocated for civil rights; decades later, she persisted through pancreatic cancer. I know if she were still with us today, she'd be right alongside me and my siblings, standing up for right in the face of today's injustices. I submit this recipe so her love, advocacy work, and nourishment can help us persist in our fight for what's right!

Submitted by: Laura Murgo

"The way I see it, no one in this country should work full-time and still live in poverty—period." - Elizabeth Warren, *This Fight is Our Fight: The Battle to Save America's Middle Class* (New York: Metropolitan Books, 2017).

" 'Nevertheless, she persisted' is an expression adopted by the feminist movement, especially in the United States. It became popular in 2017 after the United States Senate voted

to silence Senator Elizabeth Warren's objections to confir-
mation of Senator Jeff Sessions as U.S. Attorney General.
Senator Majority Leader Mitch McConnell uttered this sen-
tence during comments following the vote in an effort to de-
fend the Senate's actions and blame Warren." - Wikipedia,
"Nevertheless, she persisted," last modified October 20,
2017,
https://en.wikipedia.org/wiki/Nevertheless,_she_persisted.

MONKEY BUSINESS BREAD (OLV)

INGREDIENTS

Bread

- 4 packages refrigerated biscuit dough
- 1/2 C sugar
- 1 tsp cinnamon

Glaze

- 1 tsp cinnamon
- 1 tsp vanilla
- Sugar
- 1 stick butter

DIRECTIONS

Bread

1. Combine sugar, cinnamon. Set aside.
2. Cut biscuits into quarters.
3. Roll biscuits into sugar mixture.
4. Layer in a sprayed Bundt pan.

Glaze

1. Put 1 tsp cinnamon into an 8 oz measuring cup (microwave safe). Add enough sugar to fill cup.
2. Melt butter and add in vanilla. Stir sugar mixture into it. Pour or spoon over top of biscuits.
3. Bake 30 minutes at 350 degrees Fahrenheit.
4. Let sit about 5 minutes, then turn over onto large plate and serve warm.

Submitted by: Liberty Beth

"Donald Trump on Monday dismissed the latest employment figures, saying that he didn't 'believe' that the rate ticked down from 8.1 percent to 7.8 percent, and that the numbers

were altered through a 'lot of monkey business.'" - Katie Glueck, "Trump: 'Monkey business' on jobs," *Politico.com*, October 8, 2012.

"After, Spicer was asked about Trump's previous comments about the employment numbers being fake under President Barack Obama and if the president felt they were accurate now. 'I talked to the president prior to this,' Spicer joyfully noted, 'And he said to quote him very clearly—they may have been phony in the past but it's very real now.'" - Justin Baragona, "'It is Blatant Hypocrisy': CNN Panel Slams Trump for Saying Jobs Numbers Are 'Very Real Now,'" *MediaITE.com*, March 10, 2017.

#TAKEAKNEE NEAPOLITAN ICEBOX CAKE (OLV)

INGREDIENTS

- 10 oz chocolate graham crackers
- 1 pint each chocolate, vanilla & strawberry ice cream
- 1 tub whipped non-dairy topping
- Crushed chocolate sandwich cookies (optional)

DIRECTIONS

1. In an 8x8 glass dish or on a square platter layer graham crackers with alternating flavors of ice cream.
2. Spread whipped topping over the layers.
3. Top with crushed cookies, if desired.
4. Freeze until firm.

CONTRIBUTOR NOTES

Other types of cookies or sprinkles work well too.

Submitted by: Rachael Alice

"'I am not going to stand up to show pride in a flag for a country that oppresses black people and people of color. To me, this is bigger than football and it would be selfish on my part to look the other way. There are bodies in the street and

people getting paid leave and getting away with murder.' – Colin Kaepernick, former San Francisco 49ers quarterback, Aug. 26, 2016." - Bryan Flaherty, "From Kaepernick sitting to Trump's fiery comments: NFL's anthem protests have spurred discussion," *WashingtonPost.com*, September 24, 2017.

"For over a year I've watched lots of white Americans lose their minds in response to Colin Kaepernick and other NFL player's peaceful National Anthem protests. I've seen them question these young men's patriotism, malign their motives, attack their methods, and treat them with the kind of contempt usually reserved for serial killers and child molesters. For simply taking a knee during a football pre game in an effort to foster a conversation about the deaths of young men at the hands of police...." - John Pavlovitz, "White America, It's Time to Take a Knee," *JohnPavlovitz.com*, September 20, 2016.

"This idea that sports has always been devoid of politics is a lie." - Jemele Hill, in video posted by @TheRoot on *Twitter.com*, September 15, 2017.

IT'S THYME FOR A NEW PRESIDENT SORBET (GF, V)

Serves 2-4

INGREDIENTS

- 2/3 C water
- 1/2 C sugar or evaporated cane juice
- 8 springs fresh lemon thyme (or thyme)
- 2/3 C lemon juice fresh (3 to 4 lemons)
- 3 C blueberries, blackberries or raspberries

DIRECTIONS

1. Combine water, sugar, thyme to boil and simmer for 5 minutes.

2. Cool completely. Chill in fridge for 1 hour minimum.
3. Remove thyme sprigs. Pour sugar mixture, juice and berries into food processor or blender. Puree until smooth, transfer it into an ice cream maker and process according to the manufacture's instructions.

Submitted by: Nancy Skilton, Feel the Bern supporter.

"A nation will not survive morally or economically when so few have so much and so many have so little." - @SenSanders, *Twitter.com*, January 24, 2014.

"Eh, not a fan of the banks. They trample on the middle class. They control Washington. And why do they chain all their pens to the desks? Who's trying to steal a pen from a bank? It makes no sense!" - Colin Campbell, "Larry David hilariously parodied Bernie Sanders for 'Saturday Night Live," *BusinessInsider.com*, October 18, 2015.

PUT 'EM BEHIND BARS ALMOND BARS (OLV)
Serves 24

INGREDIENTS

- 1 C butter, softened
- 3/4 C white sugar
- 1 egg, separated
- 7 oz tube of almond paste
- 1 tsp almond extract
- 2 C flour
- 2 oz sliced almonds

DIRECTIONS

1. Preheat oven to 350 degrees Fahrenheit.

2. Cream butter and sugar and add egg yolk, almond paste and extract in food processor or a large bowl.
3. Stir in flour.
4. Pour into a greased 9x13 inch pan.
5. Beat the egg white until fluffy and brush over dough. Spread sliced almonds on top.
6. Bake for 35 minutes.
7. Let cool and cut into squares.

Submitted by: Janet Hill

"We now know, as a result of the guilty plea by Trump Campaign foreign policy advisor George Papapolous[sic], that the Russians approached the Trump campaign as early as April of 2016...[which] means that the Trump campaign was informed of Russia's involvement with stolen emails, and their intent to release them, before anyone else." - Rep. Adam Schiff, "Intel Committee Ranking Member Schiff Opening Statement at Open Hearing with Tech Companies," *Democrats-Intelligence.House.gov*, November 1, 2017.

COVFEFE TRIFLE (OLV)
Serves 12-15

INGREDIENTS

Cake

- Chocolate cake mix (any brand, the fudgier the better)
- Ingredients to prepare the cake according to the package directions

Filling

- 4 packages of chocolate instant pudding
- 6 C of milk
- 1/2 C coffee liqueur (Kalua is one brand)
- Scant 1/4 vanilla-flavored vodka (Stoli is one brand)
- Two to three 8 oz containers non-dairy whipped topping (Cool Whip is one brand), defrosted

DIRECTIONS

1. Prepare the cake according to the package directions and cut into cubes.
2. Prepare the pudding using 1 1/2 C milk per package and add the liquor to the total.
3. Add cubes of cake then a layer of whipped topping. Continue with the cake, the pudding, then the whipped topping. The final layer should be whipped topping.
4. Garnish with shaved chocolate.

CONTRIBUTOR NOTES

A variation of this is to use yellow cake, coconut cream pudding and rum.
Some prefer to poke holes in the cake and pour the Kahlua over it before cutting into cubes.
I have also assembled it in parfait cup. It's always a big hit and actually very light.

Submitted by: Representative Patricia Haddad 5th Bristol District Massachusetts

"'Despite the constant negative press covfefe,' Trump wrote, and nothing more." - William Cummings, "Trump posts vague, midnight tweet about 'negative press covfefe,'" *USAToday.com*, May 31, 2017.

COVFEFE TRIFLE (V)

Serves 12-15

INGREDIENTS

- 24 oz silken tofu
- 3 C vegan chocolate chips
- 1/2 C plus 1 TB coffee liqueur (Kalua is one brand)
- Scant 1/4 C vanilla-flavored vodka (Stoli is one brand)
- 1 TB coconut oil
- Marble or regular pound cake mix made with evaporated cane juice sweetener (or use your own vegan cake recipe)
- Nut milk of your choice
- 1 TB ground flax or chia seeds for vegan egg
- Fresh strawberries or raspberries (optional)
- 2 packages coconut or soy whipped topping (CocoWhip is one brand)

DIRECTIONS

Vegan egg (make as many as you need according to the pound cake package directions)

1. Mix your ground seeds with 3 TB water. Let sit for 15 minutes.

Pound cake

2. Follow the directions on your pound cake mix subbing the vegan egg and nut milk for eggs and milk.
3. Let cool and thinly slice.

Pudding

1. While the cake is cooking, prepare the pudding.
2. Put the chocolate chips, 1 TB of liqueur and 1 TB of coconut oil in a double boiler or microwave-proof bowl. Melt on the stove in the double boiler or use

102

the microwave, checking and stirring every 20 seconds or so.

3. Liquify the silken tofu in a blender or food processor.
4. Pour in the melted chocolate and blend completely. You may have to stop and stir periodically to make sure it's fully mixed.
5. Refrigerate for at least 2 hours.

Trifle

1. Mix the vodka and remaining coffee liqueur. Brush the cake slices generously with it.
2. Assemble your trifle starting with pudding, then cake (break up the slices to fit the shape of your trifle dish), berries and whipped topping. Repeat layers ending with whipped topping.

Submitted by: Joan Berglund

"Covfefe 1. Trying to sound smart when you don't know what you're talking about. 2. Distracting the world with typos when you've just signed a death warrant for the planet. 3. A word used to summon the Antichrist and his minions to your service." - Comment on "cofefe [sic]" definition. *UrbanDictionary.com*, May 31, 2017, https://www. urbandictionary.com/define.php?term=cofefe.

AUNT MILDRED'S IMMIGRANTS ARE WELCOME HERE CHOCOLATE CAKE (OLV)

Serves 9-16

INGREDIENTS

- 2 C all-purpose flour
- 1 tsp kosher salt
- 5 TB good powdered baking cocoa
- 1 1/2 C sugar
- 1 tsp baking soda
- 2 eggs
- 3/4 C vegetable oil
- 1 C cold water
- 1 tsp vanilla

DIRECTIONS

1. Preheat oven to 325 degrees Fahrenheit and prepare a nonstick 8x8 pan.

2. Mix all the ingredients in one large bowl: all the dry ingredients first, and then add in all of the wet ingredients.
3. Bake for 1 hour.
4. Remove from the oven and allow to cool 10 minutes before removing from the pan.
5. Frost as desired. Or not.

CONTRIBUTOR NOTES

This is my Great-Grand-Aunt Mildred's cake recipe. She was my paternal grandmother's paternal aunt, and she was a Canadian emigrant to Maine. When my dad heard I had gotten Mildred's cake recipe, he said, "I remember that cake...Aunt Mildred thought us boys could do no wrong." So clearly, he recalls this cake from his boyhood as much as he remembers a woman who I imagine must have been very loving and generous to her family, if my grandmother herself is anything to go on. Once, a pair of cousins got in to a good-natured discussion over who had the better chocolate cake recipe, so they held a cake baking competition...only to discover they both were using Mildred's recipe. Believe me it lives up to the hype, especially for how easy it is. You can make it with an afternoon's notice from easily kept kitchen staples.

Submitted by: Rachel Trousdale

Editor's note: This cake really is amazing! You can substitute GF flour easily.

"Remember, remember always that all of us, and you and I especially, are descended from immigrants and revolutionists." - Franklin D Roosevelt

45's BLUE-BURIED THE TRUTH CAKE (OLV)

Serves 9 to 16

INGREDIENTS

- 3 C flour + 1/2 C flour (to toss blueberries in)
- 3 tsp baking powder
- 1/2 tsp salt
- 1 C shortening
- 2 C sugar
- 1 tsp vanilla
- 4 eggs
- 3/4 C milk
- 2 C blueberries
- Cinnamon and sugar to sprinkle over cake as soon as it is out of the oven

DIRECTIONS

1. Preheat oven to 350 degrees Fahrenheit.
2. Cream shortening and sugar.
3. Sift together flour, baking powder and salt.
4. Add vanilla and eggs.
5. Slowly add dry, sifted ingredients and milk till mixed.
6. Remove from mixer and fold in flour coated blueberries.
7. Place in well greased baking pan.
8. Bake till inserted toothpick comes out dry.

CONTRIBUTOR NOTES

I recommend you double it. It literally disappears in my house. Freezes well. I am 68 and got this recipe 40 years ago from an even older lady. It is old fashioned goodness NOT low calorie!

I burnt my bras 50 years ago. I thought our generation would make life better for our daughters. "Life, liberty, and the pursuit of happiness" was written for women, too. I am committed to fight the battle again for my granddaughters.

Submitted by: Dragonlady Waltham

"Sad songs from blue person, very good, very meta." - Henry Alford, "Cookie Monster on the Dole," *The New Yorker*, April 17, 2017.

"DOJ not a tool for POTUS to use to go after his enemies and protect his friends. Respect rule of law and DOJ professionals. This must stop." - @SallyQYates, *Twitter.com*, November 4, 2017.

CHOCOLATE PUTIN PIE (OLV)

Serves 6-8

INGREDIENTS

- 1 store bought or homemade graham cracker crust
- 2 packages of your favorite chocolate pudding
- Whipped cream

DIRECTIONS

1. Make pudding according to package directions.
2. Pour pudding into pie shell.
3. Chill for 2 hours or overnight.
4. Top with whipped cream and serve.

Submitted by: Ann-Mary Spellman

"I hope that my story will help you understand the methods of Russian operatives in Washington and how they use U.S. enablers to achieve major foreign policy goals without disclosing their interests." - Bill Browder [driving force behind the Magnitsky Act], prepared remarks submitted to the Senate Judiciary Committee in a hearing about Foreign Agents Registration Act enforcement, July 25, 2017.

KEYstone PipeLIME PROTEST PIE (OLV)
Serves 6 to 8

INGREDIENTS

Crust:

- 1 1/2 C graham cracker crumbs
- 1/4 C sugar
- 1/4 C butter

Pie

- 5 egg yolks (save whites)
- 1 C unsweetened condensed milk
- 1/2 C lime juice from about 5 medium Key limes
- 1 tsp grated lime rinds

Topping

- 5 egg whites
- 1/2 tsp cream of tartar

- 1/2 C sugar

DIRECTIONS

Crust

1. Preheat oven to 375 degrees Fahrenheit.
2. Combine graham crackers, sugar, and butter. Mix with fingers until blended.
3. Press into a 9-inch pie plate.
4. Bake 8 to 10 minutes and cool on cooling rack.

Filling

1. Preheat oven to 350 degrees Fahrenheit.
2. Beat the yokes.
3. Slowly combine lime juice and condensed milk.
4. Pour into cooled crust.
5. Bake for 15 minutes.

Topping

1. Preheat oven to 475 degrees Fahrenheit.
2. Add cream of tartar to the egg whites. Whip egg whites until fluffy.
3. With the mixer running, add sugar and beat until firm.
4. Spread topping over pie all the way to edges.
5. Bake for 5 to 6 minutes until peaks are brown.
6. Cool and chill before serving.

CONTRIBUTOR NOTES

I found this recipe on a post card in Key West, but it called for "unsweetened condensed milk," which I assume is really evaporated milk. If you make it with sweetened condensed milk, it's too sweet. But I have also altered the recipe, using sweetened condensed milk and cutting down on the sugar in the pie overall and adding a bit more lime juice to make it tart, because I prefer tart Key Lime Pies. However, if you go with this approach, and you cut down on the sweetened condensed milk, you need to be careful that the pie doesn't turn out too runny. Let the crust refrigerate overnight and let the pie set for 8 hours before cutting into it.

I had the recipe, but no clever name for it. My brilliant brother came up with the name. When I sent him other examples, such as "Reclaiming my Thyme," he at first said, "Wow. I think I'm out of my league here," but within 30 minutes, he produced a winning name for my pie. My brother and I were both incredibly impressed with the enthusiasm and creativity of the recipe names.

Submitted by: Linda Garmon and Richard Garmon

"We are not protesters. We are protectors. We are peacefully defending our land and our ways of life. We are standing together in prayer, and fighting for what is right.'" - Iyuskin American Horse, "'We are protectors, not protesters': why I'm fighting the North Dakota pipeline," *TheGuardian.com,* August 18, 2016.

JOIN THE SHEET CAKE GRASSROOTS MOVEMENT! (GF, OLV)

Serves 24

INGREDIENTS

Sheet Cake

- 1 C butter or margarine or shortening
- 2 C granulated sugar
- 4 large eggs, room temperature
- 2 tsp pure vanilla extract
- 3 1/2 C gluten-free all-purpose flour blend (King Arthur Flour or America's Test Kitchen are best)
- 1 TB + 1 tsp baking powder
- 1 tsp baking soda
- 1 tsp xanthan gum
- 1 tsp salt

- 1 1/2 C milk (almond, soy, flax), hot

Frosting

- 6 C confectioner's sugar
- 1/2 tsp salt
- 1/2 C boiling hot water
- 2 1/2 C shortening or margarine
- 3/4 C margarine, slightly softened, cut into 1 inch pieces
- 1 TB pure vanilla extract

DIRECTIONS

Sheet cake

1. Preheat oven to 350 degrees Fahrenheit.
2. Cut parchment paper to fit the bottom of a 12x18 or sheet pan by tracing the bottom edge of the pan on the parchment paper. Grease the sides of the sheet pan and line the bottom with parchment paper, then grease the parchment paper.
3. Add margarine or butter to a large bowl and mix on low setting.
4. Microwave or heat milk on stove until hot.
5. Add 4 eggs to the mixer while it is running, scraping bowl as needed. Add vanilla extract to the mixer while it is running.
6. Sift GF flour into a large bowl and add baking powder, xanthan gum, baking soda and salt.
7. Pour half of the dry mix into the mixer while the mixer is running.
8. Pour half of the hot milk into the mixer while it is running, and then pour the rest of the dry ingredients into the mixer while it is running. Pour the rest of the milk into the mixer while it is running. Scrape sides of the bowl and mix until batter is smooth and silky.
9. Pour batter into the sheet pan and bake for 30-40 minutes. When done cool on a wire rack.

10. When cooled you may flip the cake out of pan onto another sheet pan or cardboard for frosting.

Frosting

1. In a large bowl combine sugar and salt.
2. Using a whisk, add boiling water and whisk at low speed until smooth and cool, approximately 5 minutes.
3. Add shortening or margarine.
4. Add the rest of the margarine.
5. Whisk at medium speed until smooth, approximately 3 minutes.
6. Add vanilla.
7. Increase mixing speed to medium high and whisk until light, fluffy and increased in volume, approximately 10 minutes.
8. Frosting can be covered and refrigerated for up to two weeks. To use, return to room temperature.

CONTRIBUTOR NOTES

Sheet Cake Prep Time: 20 minutes. Cook Time: 30-40 minutes. Frost top and sides of cake. Decorate top with your favorite anti-Trump quote. Eat ravenously with your like-minded friends.

Submitted by: Alissa Nourse, Harvard '99.

"I know a lot of us are feeling anxious and asking ourselves, 'What can I do?' I would urge people this Saturday instead of participating in screaming matches and potential violence, find a local business you support. Maybe a Jewish bakery or an African-American run bakery? Order a cake with the American flag on it and . . . just eat it." - Tina Fey, *Saturday Night Live*, August 17, 2017.

SNOWFLAKE-EASY-BAKE COCONUT FLAKE COOKIES (GF, OLV)

(We can't RESIST them)

INGREDIENTS

- One 15 oz bag flaked coconut
- 1 can sweetened condensed milk
- 2 tsp vanilla extract
- Good quality chocolate or small bag milk chocolate chips

DIRECTIONS

1. Preheat oven to 350 degrees Fahrenheit.
2. Mix together and shape into cookies.
3. Bake on parchment paper for ten minutes.
4. Melt chocolate chips and dip one half/cookies after they have cooled.

Submitted by: Pamela Lowell

"Snowflake: A term used to describe extremist liberals that get offended by every statement and/or belief that doesn't exactly match their own. These individuals think they are just as unique as snowflakes, when really their feelings are just as fragile." - Comment on "snowflake" definition. *UrbanDictionary.com*, September 3, 2017, https://www.urbandictionary.com/define.php?term=snowflake.

"...But if my belief in EQUITY, EMPATHY, GOODNESS and LOVE indeed makes me or people like me snowflakes, then you should know—WINTER IS COMING." - Tonya Wollschleger, Coffee Party Feminists, February 5, 2017.

"President Snowflake is feeling very unsafe in places where people are treated like people. #SamanthaBee." - @FullFrontalSamB, *Twitter.com*, February 9, 2017.

MANY WAYS TO IMPEACHMENT (FRESH BERRY NO-BAKE) PIE (OLV, GF)

Serves 6 to 8

INGREDIENTS

- 4 C fresh washed berries (blueberry/raspberry/strawberry etc)
- 1 pie shell cooked or GF graham cracker crust pie shell
- 1 C sugar (approximately)
- 1 to 2 TB cornstarch

DIRECTIONS

1. Put 1 C fresh berries and 1 C of water in saucepan.
2. Bring berries to a boil and then reduce to gentle simmer for about 20 minutes.
3. Dissolve cornstarch in small amount of water and add to berries, keep stirring until mixture thickens (okay to add a bit more cornstarch if watery—you want it thick).
4. Put rest of berries (3 C fresh) into prepared pie shell.
5. Pour cooked mixture over berries and cool in fridge.

CONTRIBUTOR NOTES

This is an incredibly easy and wonderful pie to make and serve. It captures the fresh flavors of the berries and is always a hit. My mother-in-law, Flora Shorey (a tried and true New Englander who now lives in Maine) makes if for us every summer. Flora is 85 years old and voted for Hillary, yet she's also a Susan Collins fan.

Submitted by: Pamela Lowell

"Senator Susan Collins, one of the three Republican senators who sunk the 'skinny repeal' of Obamacare on Friday, said on CNN's State of the Union Sunday that it was time to build a series of health care bills through the committee pro-

cess." - Eli Watkins, "Susan Collins: 'Go back to committee' on health care," *CNN.com*, July 30, 2017.

"Women made up the majority of the calls into Congress during the health care fight, demanding to be heard. It's clear: women won't back down." - @KamalaHarris, *Twitter.com*, August 1, 2017.

THE BAR CAN'T GET ANY LOWER CRANAPPLE BARS (OLV)

Serves 9 to 16

INGREDIENTS

- 1 C flour, plus 2 TB for thicker bars
- 1 tsp baking soda
- 1/4 tsp salt
- 1/4 tsp ground cinnamon
- 1/4 C (1/2 stick) margarine, melted
- 1/2 C of light brown sugar, firmly packed
- 1/2 C of granulated sugar
- 1 large egg
- 1 tsp vanilla extract
- 1/4 C dairy sour cream, plus 1 to 2 TB more if using extra flour for thicker bars
- 1/2 coarsely chopped fresh or frozen cranberries, slightly more if using more flour and sour cream for thicker bars
- 1/2 C peeled, cored, coarsely chopped Granny Smith or other tart green apple, slightly more if using extra flour and sour cream for thicker bars.
- Topping 1 TB granulated sugar mixed with 1/2 tsp ground cinnamon.

DIRECTIONS

1. Sift flour, baking powder, salt and cinnamon into a medium bowl OR simply whisk the dry ingredients for thicker bars.

115

2. Beat margarine, brown and granulated sugars and egg in a large bowl until mixed
3. Mix in vanilla and sour cream.
4. Add in the dry ingredients and then mix in the cranberries and apples, making sure the fruit is well coated.
5. Spoon the mixture into well-greased 8x8x2 pan. Make certain the mixture is spread evenly into the corners and even out the middle.
6. Sprinkle the topping over the mixture.
7. Bake in middle of oven at 350 degrees Fahrenheit, for about 30 minutes, or until the sides pull back and top springs back when touched.
8. Cool in pan then slice into bars.

CONTRIBUTOR NOTES

The original recipe called for less flour and fruit. I decided to make it slightly tarter, because I lost my sense of taste for sugar in a car accident, and to make the bars thicker for easier transporting. My family gobbled the new version down before it even finished cooling and is now a family traditional dessert for the holidays. It's traveled with me down south and was an instant winner and has crossed cultures as well.

Submitted by: Kerrie May

"There is a law of nature emerging from the White House. If a bar is low, it can always go lower.... And yet, now that the Mooch [Anthony Scaramucci, Trump's Director of Communications from July 21-31, 2017] has lowered the bar yet again to the level of expletives and unprintables and asterisks, Spicer seems like something out of Gone with the Wind.*"* - Nesrine Malik, "Spicer who? Anthony Scaramucci shows that in Trump's world the bar can always go lower," *NewStatesman.com*, July 28, 2017.

TOUGH COOKIES (V)

Makes about 2 dozen cookies

INGREDIENTS

- 2 C flour
- 1 tsp baking soda
- 1/2 tsp salt
- 1 C non-dairy chocolate chips
- 1/4 C brown sugar or evaporated cane juice
- 3/4 C white sugar or evaporated cane juice
- 1/2 C + 2 TB non-dairy margarine such as Earth Balance brand
- 2 tsp vanilla
- 2 1/2 TB soymilk or other non-dairy milk

DIRECTIONS

1. Preheat the oven to 350 degrees Fahrenheit.
2. In a large bowl mix the flour, baking soda, and salt. Make a well in the center and set aside.
3. In a saucepan, melt the margarine over low heat. Stir in the sugars and mix well. Add the vanilla and soymilk and stir again.
4. Add the wet ingredients to the dry ingredients and combine until fully blended.
5. Spoon onto ungreased cookie sheet.
6. Bake for 9 minutes or until the cookies are a little softer then you want them to be—they will harden a bit as they cool.
7. When done baking, cool on wire racks. If the cookies break when transferring to the racks, let them sit on the cookie sheet for a few minutes before transferring.

CONTRIBUTOR NOTES

Since this recipe doesn't contain eggs if you're day is super stressful you can safely eat the dough! Why bother baking?

Submitted by: Blakely Sullivan

"Women racked up victories across the country on Tuesday, and are being credited with the Democrats' big night overall. It is a testament to the remarkable explosion of women candidates who have entered the political stage since Donald Trump was elected president one year ago.... 'This is huge,' said Stephanie Schriock, president of Emily's List, the political group that backs female Democratic candidates who support abortion rights. 'This is how we build momentum for 2018. Women are going to lead the way.'" -Mary Jordan, Karen Tumulty and Michael Alison Chandler, "Women racked up victories across the country Tuesday. It may be only the beginning," *WashingtonPost.com,* November 8, 2017.

PETRA'S TROLL HOUSE COOKIES (OLV)

Makes 18 to 24 cookies

INGREDIENTS

Dry ingredients

- 1 1/8 - 1 1/4 C sifted all-purpose flour
- 1/2 tsp salt
- 1/2 tsp baking powder
- 1/2 C real chocolate chips (Ghirardelli is good)
- 1/3 C pecans or walnut pieces (optional)
-

Sugars

- 4 TB packed brown sugar
- 8 TB white sugar

Wet ingredients

- 1 large beaten egg, preferably room temperature
- 1/2 C vegetable oil, grapeseed is best, canola will do
- 1/2 tsp real vanilla extract

DIRECTIONS

1. Preheat oven to 350 degrees. Line two cookie sheets with parchment.
2. Combine the dry ingredients (flour, salt, baking powder) in one bowl.
3. Combine the sugars in another bowl.
4. Whisk together wet ingredients in another larger bowl.
5. Add sugars to wet ingredients. Mix thoroughly with a wooden spoon. Add remaining dry ingredients. Mix thoroughly.
6. Fold in chocolate chips, and 1/3 C pecans or walnut pieces (optional).
7. Put a heaping tsp of the batter in your hand and roll it into a ball. Place the ball on the parchment lined cookie sheet, then press the ball with the palm of your hand until it is flat and round. Place the next ball 2 inches from the last and press. Repeat till sheet is full.
8. Bake 8-12 minutes (ovens vary) until the cookies are golden brown. If they are wrinkled, you needed more flour; your egg may have been extra-large. If they were brown on the edges and raw in the middle, lower the oven temp to 325 next time and bake longer. Keep on tweaking—it'll be worth it!

CONTRIBUTOR NOTES

The secret to these being especially light chocolate chip cookies is in the small batches and brown to white sugar ratio. If you want more cookies (this makes 18-24), don't double the recipe; make two separate batches instead.

Submitted by: Petra Breen

"It looks like Russia hired internet trolls to pose as pro-Trump Americans. Russia's troll factories were, at one point, likely being paid by the Kremlin to spread pro-Trump propaganda on social media." - Natasha Bertrand, "It looks like

Russia hired internet trolls to pose as pro-Trump American,"
BusinessInsider.com, July 27, 2016.

SETH MOULT-EN LAVA CAKE (OLV)

Serves 4

INGREDIENTS

- 1/2 C of unsalted butter (for cake)
- 1 TB or less of unsalted butter (for buttering ramekins)
- 4 oz high-quality bittersweet or semisweet chocolate
- 4 large eggs
- 1/2 C sugar
- 2 tsp flour (for cake)
- 4 pinches of flour (for dusting ramekins)

DIRECTIONS

1. Preheat oven to 450 degrees Fahrenheit.
2. Chop the chocolate into small pieces.
3. Melt the 1/2 C butter in a medium size microwave-safe bowl in the microwave.
4. Add the chocolate to the bowl of hot butter and stir until melted.
5. In a separate bowl, mix the whites and yolks of 2 eggs, plus just the yolks of 2 more eggs.
6. Add the sugar to the egg mixture and beat or whisk until thick, approximately 1 minute.
7. Add the egg mixture and 2 tsp of flour to the melted chocolate. Beat until ingredients are combined.
8. Butter and lightly flour the entire interior surface area of four 4 oz ramekins to prevent the cakes from sticking, tapping out excess flour.
9. Divide the cake batter among the ramekins.
10. Ramekins can be refrigerated for up to 3 hours (then brought back to room temperature before baking) or baked immediately.

11. Put the ramekins on a rimmed baking sheet and bake for 7 to 9 minutes. Cakes are ready when they've puffed up slightly, their tops are beginning to set, and they still jiggle slightly when shaken. (Cakes are better under baked than over baked).
12. Remove cakes from oven and let sit for 1 minute.
13. Place a plate on top of the ramekin and - using a potholder - carefully invert the cake onto the plate. Let the cake sit for 10 seconds before lifting up the ramekin. Serve immediately.

CONTRIBUTOR NOTES

Cakes can be served with ice cream, sorbet, or whipped cream.

Molten chocolate lava cake is my favorite dessert in the world. I've renamed this recipe Seth Moult-en Lava Cake in honor of Massachusetts Sixth District Congressman Seth Moulton.

Submitted by: Seven Sister Resister

"Congressman Seth Moulton (D-Mass.) sees similarities between the quick rise of Donald Trump today and Adolf Hitler in the 1930s. 'When you're in politics, one of the cardinal rules is you never say what I'm about to say,' the former Iraq veteran said in a taped conversation with the Boston Globe on Wednesday. Then he said it: 'People should read the history of how Germany elected Hitler.'" - Hanna Trudo, "Rep. Seth Moulton compares Trump to Hitler," *Politico.com*, March 23, 2016.

W[H]INEY GOP BISCUITS (V)

Makes 5 dozen biscuits

INGREDIENTS

- 1 C red wine (if vegan, choose vegan wine)
- 1 C sugar or evaporated cane juice, plus extra for dipping
- 1 C oil
- 3 tsp baking powder
- 1/4 tsp salt
- 5 C sifted flour (approximately)
- 1 C crushed walnuts (optional)

DIRECTIONS

1. Preheat oven to 375 degrees Fahrenheit.
2. Mix wine, sugar, oil, baking powder and salt.
3. Add crushed walnuts (if you are using them).
4. Gradually add flour to make a moist dough.
5. Scoop off about slightly more than 1 tsp of dough. Roll into balls the size of a walnut, or shape into rings or twists.
6. Dip rolled dough into the extra sugar to coat.
7. Place biscuits on baking tray covered with parchment paper.
8. Bake about 20 minutes.
9. Do not open oven door for the first 15 minutes.

Submitted by: Carrie M.

"Speaking at a Rotary Club meeting in Kentucky Monday, Sen. Maj. Leader Mitch McConnell whined and complained about the impression people have that the Senate hasn't accomplished much under his leadership during the Trump administration." - Chris Pandolfo, "Mark Levin flays Mitch McConnell for whining about Trump," *ConservativeReview.com*, August 9, 2017.

TINY HANDS SCONES (OLV)

INGREDIENTS

- 2 C all-purpose flour
- 1/3 C sugar
- 1 tsp baking powder
- 1/4 tsp baking soda
- 1/2 tsp salt
- 8 TB unsalted butter very cold
- 1/2 C dried cranberries (or dried blueberries)
- 1/2 C chopped pecans
- 1/2 C sour cream
- 1 egg

DIRECTIONS

1. Preheat oven to 400 degrees Fahrenheit and set rack to lower middle position.
2. Mix flour and dry ingredients. Grate butter into flour mixture using a box grater. Use fingers to work butter into mixture until it resembles a coarse meal.
3. Stir in nuts and cranberries.
4. In separate bowl whisk sour cream and egg until smooth. With a fork stir this into the flour mixture until dough comes together. With your hands press the dough against the side of the bowl to form a ball. Do not overwork dough or it will become tough.
5. Place on floured surface and pat into an 8 inch circle about 3/4 inch thick. Using a sharp knife cut circle into 8 triangles.
6. Sprinkle with sugar and place on a parchment lined cookie sheet.
7. Bake until golden brown, about 15 to 17 minutes. Serve warm.

Submitted by: Karen Nourse

"Finally, there's proof that Donald Trump has small hands. He has smaller hands than 85 percent of American men.... [The Hollywood Reporter] editors have printed a life-size image of Trumps hands, which they created based on a

bronzed handprint hanging in the New York branch of Madame Tussauds Wax Museum.... Are Trump's hands really that tiny? No—at 7.25 inches long, they're slightly smaller than average." - David Moye, "Finally, There's Proof That Donald Trump Has Small Hands," *HuffingtonPost.com*, August 3, 2016.

RUSSIAN CAPER PEANUT BUTTER BARS (OLV)

INGREDIENTS

- 2 C graham cracker crumbs (can use GF)
- 2 C confectioners' sugar
- 1 C smooth peanut butter, not natural
- 1 1/2 C dark chocolate chips
- 4 TB peanut butter

DIRECTIONS

1. Mix graham cracker crumbs, confectioners' sugar and 1 C peanut butter together.
2. Press into bottom of ungreased 9 x 13 pan.
3. In metal bowl over simmering water (or in microwave) melt chocolate chips with 4 TB of peanut butter, stirring until smooth.
4. Spread over graham cracker mixture.
5. Refrigerate for at least two hours before cutting into squares.

Submitted by: Karen Nourse

"Because of Putin's fears that fidget spinners are a U.S. ploy to undermine him, 'Russia is banning fidget spinners,' [Trevor] Noah said, 'And just like that, there goes Russia's reputation as a fun country.'" -" Trevor Noah notes that Putin sees U.S. meddling in Russia's presidential election, via fidget spinners," *TheWeek.com*, July 20, 2017.

MR. TURTLE SINFUL BROWNIES (OLV)

INGREDIENTS

- 50 caramels
- 1/2 C evaporated milk
- 1 package German chocolate cake mix
- 3/4 C melted butter
- 1/3 C evaporated milk
- 6 oz chocolate chips

DIRECTIONS

1. Preheat oven to 350 degrees Fahrenheit.
2. Melt caramels in 1/2 C evaporated milk in a double boiler.
3. Mix cake batter, butter, and 1/3 evaporated milk together.
4. Place 1/2 batter in a 9x13 pan. Bake 6-10 minutes.
5. Remove and cool slightly.
6. Sprinkle chocolate chips over batter, then pour melted caramel mixture over chips.
7. Add rest of batter on top in "patties" or spread.
8. Bake 20 minutes more.

Submitted by: Pamela Lowell

"In the pantheon of least favorite turtles, there is one who is far and away the most hated — far below surfer-turtle Crush from 'Finding Nemo,' the turtle from 'Discworld' who holds up the planet, and all four Teenage Mutant Ninjas. That would be, of course, Sen. Mitch McConnell." - Constance Gibbs, "Happy Turtle Day, Sen. Mitch 'Turtle' McConnell!" *NewYorkDailyNews.com,* May 23, 2017.

OBAMA, WE MISS YOU, TIRAMISU (OLV)

Serves 4

INGREDIENTS

- 5 egg yolks
- 3 egg whites
- 2/3 C sugar
- 2 to 3 TB rum
- 300 grams ladyfingers (usually 1 package with 3 sections of ladyfingers or 1 1/2 with 2 sections)
- 2 C espresso coffee
- 1 large container (500 grams) of mascarpone cheese (or 2 small ones)
- Dark cocoa (I use Hershey special dark)

DIRECTIONS

1. In a kitchen mixer, mix sugar, rum and egg yolks together until smooth and light yellow in color.
2. Add mascarpone cheese and mix until well incorporated in the yolk/ sugar mixture.
3. Separately whip the egg whites until firm.
4. Gently fold the egg whites into the mascarpone mixture.
5. Lightly soak the ladyfingers in a little bit of espresso and lay them on a pan forming a layer.
6. Add half of the mascarpone mixture in top of the ladyfinger layer.
7. Form another layer of ladyfingers.
8. Put remaining mascarpone mixture on top.
9. Finish by dusting cocoa powder on top.
10. Refrigerate for at least 1-2 hours before serving.

Submitted by: Turi Curi

"A change is brought about because ordinary people do extraordinary things." - Barack Obama, Presidential Nomination acceptance speech, August 28, 2008.

"My fellow Americans, it has been the honor of my life to serve you. I won't stop: in fact, I will be right there with you, as a citizen, for all my days that remain. For now, whether you're young or young at heart, I do have one final ask of you as your president—the same thing I asked when you took

a chance on me eight years ago. I am asking you to believe. Not in my ability to bring about change—but in yours…Yes We Can. Yes We Did. Yes We Can." - President Obama, Farewell speech, January 10, 2017.

DUMP TRUMP BARS (OLV)

Makes 40 bars

INGREDIENTS

- 1 C butter (2 sticks)
- 1/2 tsp salt
- 4 eggs
- 1 tsp vanilla
- 1 entire box of light brown sugar (yes you read that correctly—we need lots of sugar to get through this administration)
- 1/2 C chopped nuts
- 1/2 C chocolate chips
- 2 C flour
- 1 tsp baking powder
- 1 C flaked coconut

DIRECTIONS

1. Dump first 4 ingredients into the top of a double boiler.
2. Stir and heat until the butter is melted.
3. Remove from heat.
4. Dump the rest of the ingredients in and beat well.
5. Pour into a greased 8 x 13 x 2 pan.
6. Bake at 350 for 40 minutes, cool and remove. Slice.

CONTRIBUTOR NOTES

This is an awfully sweet dessert. Maybe you can give them away for the holidays? Or to your relatives who haven't yet put on the Trump Twenty? They also freeze well for nights when the news is just too depressing to handle without some emotional eating to get you through (not that we've ever done that).

Submitted by: Pamela Lowell

"Dump Trump Movement crashes and burns ahead of GOP convention. RNC Convention rules committee throttles effort to deny Trump the nomination." - S. V. Date and Igor Bobic, "Dump Trump Movement Crashes And Burns Ahead Of GOP Convention," *HuffingtonPost.com,* July 14, 2017.

ORANGE FOOL (OLV)

INGREDIENTS

- Juice of 6 oranges
- 6 eggs, well beaten
- 1 pint of cream
- 1/4 pound of sugar
- A little cinnamon
- A little nutmeg
- A piece of butter

DIRECTIONS

1. Take the juice of six oranges and six eggs well beaten, a pint of cream, a quarter of a pound of sugar, a little cinnamon and nutmeg; mix all together, and keep stirring over a slow fire, till it is thick, then put in a little piece of butter, and keep stirring till cold, and dish it up.

CONTRIBUTOR NOTES

George Washington could not have imagined that his favorite dessert would succeed him as president 220 years after he retired to Mount Vernon, yet an "Orange Fool" currently occupies the oval office.

This custard-like dessert was an expensive treat in colonial times because oranges had to be imported from the Caribbean. So, an Orange Fool would only have been enjoyed by the wealthiest people in 1797. As far as we know today, Trump Tower and the White House are the only places you can find an Orange Fool on a regular basis.

This recipe comes from Hannah Glasse's The Art of Cookery Made Plain and Easy, published in 1747. Today, Martha Washington's copy resides in the library at Mount Vernon. Colonial recipe books were not overly specific, so you might have to judge a few ingredients for yourself. Or google "Orange Fool" for an updated recipe. You might also find the rantings of a few snowflakes that think this recipe is all about the Trump Tower version of Orange Fool!

Submitted by: Marlene Cook

"'Clearly a fake desert [sic] story poking fun at the physical characteristics of a national hero.'" - Talia Lavin, "The Eighteenth-Century Custard Recipe That Enraged Trump Supporters," *NewYorker.com*, September 8, 2017.

LADY LOUISE'S JEWELED GEL MOLD (V)

INGREDIENTS

- 2 C of naturally red juice like pomegranate, cranberry or raspberry
- 1 C of pineapple juice
- 9 oz container of non-dairy whipped topping (Coco Whip is one brand)
- 3 1/2 tsp agar powder, separated (this recipe is written for agar powder, not flakes)

DIRECTIONS

1. Add 1 1/2 tsp of agar to the 2 C of red juice in a saucepan. Whisk thoroughly. Bring to a boil while still whisking. Reduce to a simmer and continue to heat with stirring for about 5 minutes.

2. Pour into a greased loaf pan and chill for about 2 hours.
3. While the first batch of gel is chilling, remove the whipped topping about 30 minutes before you want to use it to warm it to room temperature (cold topping will start to solidify the agar too quickly and you'll get lumps).
4. Grease a 6 cup gel mold.
5. Cut the red gel into cubes when it is completely firm and carefully remove the cubes from the pan with a spatula. Keep handy.
6. Add the pineapple juice and 2 tsp of agar powder to a saucepan. Whisk thoroughly. Bring to a boil. Reduce to a simmer and very quickly stir the whipped topping into the pan, whisking thoroughly. Packaged non-dairy topping should hold up to the heat okay. Let simmer for about 5 minutes while whisking constantly.
7. Pour a little into your mold, add a few red cubes and repeat this process until the mold is full.
8. Chill for about 2 hours.
9. To demold, soak the mold in a couple of inches of warm water briefly and then put a serving plate over the top and carefully invert.

CONTRIBUTOR NOTES

Since I don't eat beef, I figured that meant I don't eat hoof either. So, I decided to experiment with a vegan agar gel mold. Agar is firmer than gelatin and sets up faster, so you need to work quickly when assembling it. The usual gelatin "crown jewels dessert" technique of stirring the whipped topping into the cooled gel after it has started to solidify won't work, you'll get lumps. You need to stir the topping right into the hot pan. You can reverse engineer this into a non-vegan recipe by looking up "crown jewels" or "stained glass" gelatin dessert.

For the winter holidays, you can do half red and half green colored cubes. You'll probably need to add food coloring to a light-colored juice to get a sufficiently bright green. You can also make it in a graham cracker pie shell or in a trifle dish lined with ladyfingers.

Submitted by: Joan Berglund

"As one does when one is marrying a person whose boss ran for president on a populist platform that involved blaming 'a global power structure' for 'the economic decisions that have robbed our working class,' Linton recently sat down with Town & Country to talk about all the jewels she'll be wearing for the big occasion, most of which, obviously, are diamonds." - Bess Levin, "Steven Mnuchin's Fiancee Accidentally Makes a Case for Higher Taxes," *VanityFair.com*, June 23, 2017.

"Your life looks cute." - @LouiseLinton, *Instagram.com*, August 21, 2017.

CONSPIRACY CAKE WITH INDICTMENT ICING (OLV)

Serves 12-20

INGREDIENTS

Cake

- One 20 oz can crushed pineapple
- 2 C white whole-wheat or whole wheat pastry flour
- 2 tsp baking soda
- 1/2 tsp salt
- 1 1/2 tsp pumpkin pie spice
- 3 extra large eggs
- 1 C organic granulated sugar or evaporated cane juice
- 3/4 cup nonfat kefir
- 1/2 cup canola oil
- 1 tsp vanilla extract
- 1/2 C organic brown or raw sugar

- 2 cups grated beets
- 1/2 cup chopped pecans
- 1/2 cup dried cranberries
- A few drops of red food coloring (optional)

Frosting

- 12 oz Neufchâtel cream cheese, softened
- 1/3 C confectioners' sugar, sifted
- 1 1/2 tsp vanilla extract
- 2 TB pineapple juice
- A few drops yellow food coloring (optional)

DIRECTIONS

Cake

1. Preheat oven to 350 degrees Fahrenheit. Grease a 9x13 inch baking pan with cooking spray or coconut oil.
2. Drain pineapple through a strainer over a bowl. You'll have to press on the solids some to get all the juice out. Reserve both pineapple and the juice.
3. Whisk the dry ingredients (flour, pumpkin pie spice, baking soda and salt) together in a medium bowl.
4. Whisk eggs, sugar, kefir, oil, vanilla and 1/4 C of the pineapple juice in a large bowl until blended. Stir in pineapple and beets. Add the food coloring, if using. Add the dry ingredients and mix until blended. Stir in the nuts and cranberries. Pour the batter into the prepared pan.
5. Bake the cake about 40 to 45 minutes, until the center springs back when touched lightly and a toothpick inserted in the center comes out clean.
6. Let cool completely on a wire rack for about 30 minutes. Take the cream cheese out to soften while the cake cools.

Frosting

1. Beat cream cheese, confectioners' sugar, 2 TB of re-served pineapple juice and yellow food coloring (if using) in a mixing bowl with an electric mixer until creamy and evenly colored. Spread the frosting over the cooled cake in the pan or loosen and put a serving tray of the top and carefully invert to demold.
2. Reserve the remaining pineapple juice for another use (Pina Colluda?).

CONTRIBUTOR NOTES

This is a little on the nutritious side for a dessert, but we have to keep up our strength. I promise it's still delicious. Whole wheat pastry flour is the best choice for whole grain cakes if you want the texture to be as close to traditional white flour as possible. It's made with a soft grain white wheat. White whole wheat is made with a hard grain white wheat but still works well. It's what I used, and it was still very moist and soft. Regular (hard red grain) whole wheat would have the most earthy chewiness, but is also usable. It's a matter of preference, and what you can find in your area. The cake will be a little red from the beets, but if you want a more lurid red-velvet red, you'll have to add some food coloring. You can use natural (usually tumeric-based) food coloring for the frosting, but the natural reds are often beet-based and turn brown with cooking.

Submitted by: Joan Berglund

"At the end of a wild Monday, three of President Donald Trump's associates were indicted on criminal charges. Two pleaded not guilty in federal court, and one pleaded guilty to making false statements to the FBI about his contacts with Russian officials." - Rebecca Harrington, "MUELLER MONDAY: Here's everything we learned about the Paul Manafort, Rick Gates, George Papadopoulos indictments," *BusinessInsider.com,* October 31, 2017.

WE LIVE IN THE UPSIDE-DOWN PINEAPPLE CAKE
Serves 15

INGREDIENTS

Topping

- 1/2 C (1 stick) butter
- 1 1/2 C brown sugar, tightly packed
- 9 pineapple rings
- 9 to 18 maraschino cherries

Cake
- 2/3 C butter
- 1 1/3 C sugar
- 2 tsp vanilla extract
- 4 eggs
- 3 1/3 C flour
- 4 tsp baking powder
- 1 1/3 C milk

DIRECTIONS

1. Preheat oven to 350 degrees Fahrenheit.
2. Add butter and brown sugar to 9x13 inch sheet pan. Place in oven while preparing batter.
3. Cream butter in large mixing bowl. Add sugar gradually and beat well. Add eggs and vanilla, beat until light and fluffy.
4. Mix flour and baking powder. Add flour/baking powder mixture alternately with milk to the butter/sugar/egg mixture, and beat until smooth.
5. Remove pan with topping from oven; stir butter and brown sugar to distribute evenly in pan.
6. Place pineapple rings in rows in the pan with the butter and sugar mixture. Place a cherry in the center of each pineapple ring, and if you'd like you can also place them in between where the pineapples meet.
7. Slowly pour cake batter over pineapples and cherries.

8. Bake 35-40 minutes or until toothpick inserted into center comes out clean.
9. Place a serving plate over the top of your pan and invert cake while hot.

Submitted by: Elisha Fielding

"'Like the main characters in Stranger Things, *we are now stuck in the Upside Down, right is wrong, up is down, black is white,' [R.I. Rep David] Cicilline said.... 'We have a president unlike any we have ever known and like Mike, Dustin, Lucas and Eleven we must remain focused on the task at hand and hold the administration accountable, so we can escape from our own version of the Upside Down.'"* - Mary Bowerman, "Congressman compares Trump administration to 'Upside Down' in 'Stranger Things,'" *USAToday.com,* February 17, 2017.

"If there was one decision I would overrule, it would be Citizens United. I think the notion that we have all the democracy that money can buy strays so far from what our democracy is supposed to be." - Supreme Court Justice Ruth Bader Ginsburg, interview by Jeffrey Rosen, *New Republic*, September 28, 2014.

"[N]either Ivanka nor Jared should be [in the administration] in the first place. They were not elected, they are likely violating a number of laws ranging from emoluments to security clearance improprieties, they have no qualifications for their jobs, and they wield enough influence that an offhand remark can lead to a bombing and a handbag line can lead to a change in foreign policy, which is a horrifying way for an administration to function," - Sarah Kendzior, "The tale of the dictator's daughter and her prince," *TheCorrespondent.com,* April 25, 2017.

AWKWARD HANDSHAKES AND OTHER BEVERAGES

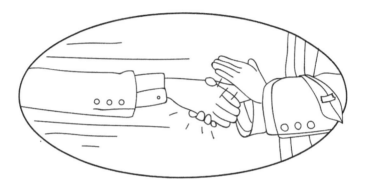

NASTY MANGO LASSI (OLV OR V)

Serves 2

INGREDIENTS

- 1 C frozen mango chunks
- 1 C vanilla yogurt
- 1/4 C coconut milk, or milk of choice
- 2 TB agave syrup
- Pinch of cinnamon
- 1 TB crushed pistachios for garnish, optional

DIRECTIONS

1. Place first five ingredients in blender.
2. Blend until smooth.
3. Top with pistachios if desired.

CONTRIBUTOR NOTES

Submitted by: Lois Caldrello

"What I meant when I said that Hillary Clinton had made the world ready for Hillary Clinton is that I recognized her as a woman who had whacked the weeds to blaze her own trail, who had always stood up again after she was told to sit down, who had persisted, and persisted, and persisted, nevertheless. What I meant is that a woman like this was finally going to win. Someday she will." - Cheryl Strayed, "Cheryl Strayed: Someday, a 'Nasty' Woman Like Hillary Clinton Will Win," *Time.com*, October 3, 2017.

ICED COVFEFE—I MEAN COFFEE—ICE CUBES (GF, V)

INGREDIENTS

- 1 pot freshly brewed coffee
- Ice cube tray

DIRECTIONS

1. Brew a pot of covfefe, I mean coffee.
2. Allow covfefe to cool.
3. Pour cooled covfefe into ice cube trays and chill until frozen.

CONTRIBUTOR NOTES

Use these covfefe ice cubes in your homemade iced covfefe to keep it from getting diluted by water! This will allow you to get fully caffeinated after staying up too late the night before watching the news and making signs for rallies

Submitted by: South Shore Blue

"Let's argue. Let's have the great American debate about the role of government and the best policies for the country. It's fun. It's activism. It makes the country better when we have those debates. And your country needs you. It needs all of us. But two things disqualify you from this process: You can't threaten to shoot people and you have to stop making stuff up." - Rachel Maddow, MSNBC's *The Rachel Maddow Show,* April 2, 2010.

DRAIN THE SWAMP SMOOTHIE (GF, V)

INGREDIENTS

- 2 frozen bananas
- 1/4 - 1/2 C ice cubes
- 2/3 C soy or almond milk
- 1 C raw spinach (about two handfuls if you have small hands!)
- 1 TB flax seeds
- 1/8 tsp mint extract

DIRECTIONS

1. In a blender, blend all ingredients together until smooth.

Submitted by: Blakely Sullivan

"It's disappointing that the man who promised to 'drain the swamp' just took a massive step away from transparency.... This week, we sued the Trump administration to make sure they would continue to release the logs. It looks like we'll see them in court." - Noah Bookbinder, "CREW Statement on White House Refusal to Release Visitor Logs," *Citizens-ForEthics.org,* April 14, 2017.

"So it seems a more accurate three-word campaign promise would have been, 'Run! Swamp monsters!'" - Seth Meyers, *Late Night with Seth Meyers*, May 24, 2017.

WHAT HAPPENED HOT CHOCOLATE (OLV)

INGREDIENTS

- 8 C of dried milk
- 1 -11 oz jar of powdered coffee whitener (Coffee-mate is one brand)
- 1 lb box of powdered chocolate milk mix (Nestle Quick is one brand)
- 1 C of sugar

- Dash of salt

DIRECTIONS

1. Combine all ingredients in a large storage container.
2. Stir or shake to mix them up.
3. Put 1/4 C of the mix in a C and fill with boiling water.

CONTRIBUTOR NOTES

Variations, depending upon the news cycle: add peppermint Schnapps and top with peppermint whipped cream (Target sells it); If it's a trash Hillary news cycle or kill-our-healthcare kind of day add flavored vodka (Stoli's Salted Caramel Vodka is one brand), top with whipped cream and drizzles of caramel.

This is my husband's family recipe which we make each year. Make sure your storage container is airtight. Kids like to stir this with peppermint sticks at Christmas time (without the alcohol, of course.)

Submitted by: Sherri Nordhaus

"Hillary Clinton won the popular vote again, but this time it's not at the ballot box. "What Happened," *Clinton's campaign memoir about her presidential run against Donald Trump, sold 167,000 hardcover copies in the United States in its first week. That is the largest first week sales for a hardcover nonfiction book since 2012's* "No Easy Day" *by Mark Owen. Clinton's memoir sold more than 300,000 copies across all formats, which includes hardcover, e-book, CD and digital audio books."* - Frank Pallotta, "Hillary Clinton's *'What Happened'* sees big sales in its first week," *CNN.com,* September 20, 2017.

MUELLER'S HOT ON THE TRAIL MULLED APPLE CIDER (GF, V)

INGREDIENTS

- 6 C apple cider
- 1 tsp cinnamon
- 1/4 tsp nutmeg
- 1/4 tsp cloves
- 1/4 tsp allspice
- Chopped apple sliced very thin including peel
- Lemon or orange peels (optional)

DIRECTIONS

1. Put all ingredients in small saucepan for 10-15 minutes. Can adjust spices to taste. Add 1 to 2 TB of chopped apple into mug right before serving.

CONTRIBUTOR NOTES

Perfect for those fall nights when you're needing a mug of hope, mulling over what resistance activity you'll be doing tomorrow, and dreaming about subpoenas, charges, indictments and impeachments.

Submitted by: Muellercrush

"Mueller has his pick of some of the top lawyers in the country. 'If you're a prosecutor, this is what you dream of—getting a case like this,' says Peter Zeidenberg, who prosecuted I. Lewis 'Scooter' Libby, Vice President Dick Cheney's chief of staff." - Tom Schoenberg and David Voreacos, "Mueller's Dream Team Gears Up," *Bloomberg.com*, June 19, 2017.

"A former federal prosecutor who helped take down mob boss John Gotti said the indictments released Monday by special counsel Robert Mueller are a strong indication that his team is looking to play hardball with other witnesses for the remainder of the Russia probe." - Todd Shepherd, "For-

mer assistant US attorney: Robert Mueller indictments send tough message to other witnesses," *WashingtonExaminer.com*, October 30, 2017.

FIFTH AVENUE SHOTS (OR, I'VE BEEN DRINKING DAILY SINCE NOVEMBER)

ELECTION NIGHT VIN CHAUD

Serves 6

INGREDIENTS

- 1 bottle of red wine (choose something with some sweetness, like Grenache or Syrah)
- 1 whole star anise
- 3 green cardamom pods
- 3 whole cloves
- Generous pinch of freshly ground black pepper
- 1/4 C mild-flavored, raw, local honey
- 1/4 C plum brandy or eau-de-vie

DIRECTIONS

1. Put the star anise, green cardamom pods, and whole cloves in a reusable linen spice bag for ease.
2. Heat all ingredients EXCEPT the brandy in a crock pot for 3 hours.
4. Before serving, add the brandy to the warm mulled wine in the crock pot.
3. Ladle out in to mugs to serve.
4. Refrigerate any leftover wine in an air-tight vessel and reheat for a pick-me-up the next morning.

Submitted by: Rachel Trousdale

"This is painful, and it will be for a long time. But I want you to remember this: Our campaign was never about one person or even one election. It was about the county we love, and about building an America that's hopeful, inclusive and big hearted...So now our responsibility as citizens is to keep doing our part to build that better, stronger, fairer America we seek." - Hillary Clinton, General presidential election concession speech, November 9, 2016.

HUMPTY TRUMPTY FELL OFF THE HARVEY WALLBANGERS

Serves 1

INGREDIENTS

- 1 to 1 1/2 oz vodka
- 4 oz orange juice
- 1 C ice
- 1/2 oz Galliano
- Orange slices for garnish

- Tall, 10-14 oz glasses (Collins glass)

DIRECTIONS

1. Pour vodka and orange juice into a tall glass, add ice and stir.
2. Layer the Galliano on top by pouring slowly (can pour over a spoon).
3. Garnish with orange slices and hope for the best!

Submitted by: Lee McEvoy Robért

During Hurricane Harvey, Lee posted this drink on her FB page and we asked for the recipe; the name was her idea. After Harvey, Lee's extended family (and many other heroes) rescued people who had flooded in Port Arthur and Houston areas. Her family members were also survivors of Katrina. Lee said, "Our neighborhood was badly damaged (by Katrina) but got up and running with tons of help. I cleaned out so many homes and businesses that my body ached."

"He later described the victims to reporters and called the historic hurricane a wonderful thing for the world to watch. He also wished everyone a good time as they try to rebuild their lives." - Desire Thompson, "Trump Says Hurricane Harvey Is Great For The Country To Watch, Tells Victims To Have A Good Time," *Vibe.com*, September 2, 2017.

BITTERSWEET ORANGE-RUSSIAN FRIENDSHIP

Serves 1

INGREDIENTS

- 1 1/2 oz vodka
- 1/2 oz good quality orange curacao or orange liqueur (such as Cointreau or Grand Marnier)
- 4 shakes of orange bitters or to taste
- Enough black unsweetened iced chai (such as Twinging's Chai) and orange juice to fill a 10-14 oz highball glass

DIRECTIONS

1. Add ice, vodka and orange liqueur to highball glass.
2. Fill with 1/2 orange juice and 1/2 iced chai.
3. Add about 4 healthy shakes of orange bitters.

CONTRIBUTOR NOTES

This was inspired by the '70s Friendship Tea recipe (using powdered orange drink and powdered ice tea mix) that my grandmother liked to serve iced at her pool parties around the time of Apollo-Soyuz. The current administration's fondness for Putin isn't quite the detente we were envisioning back then.

Submitted by: Joan Berglund

[Rob Goldstone:] "This is obviously very high level and sensitive information but is part of Russia and its government's support for Mr. Trump."

[Donald Trump, Jr:] "If it's what you say I love it." - Rosalind S. Helderman and John Wagner, "Donald Trump Jr. was told campaign meeting would be with 'Russian government attorney,' according to emails," *WashingtonPost.com*, July 11, 2017.

IMPEACH-MINT MOJITO
INGREDIENTS

Serves 1

- 2 oz fresh lime juice
- 1 oz simple syrup
- 2 oz white rum
- 8 mint leaves
- One 12 oz can seltzer (plain, raspberry, lemon or lime work well)

DIRECTIONS

1. Start by making simple syrup. In a small saucepan, bring 1 C sugar and 1 C water to a boil. Simmer until the sugar is dissolved, about 3 minutes. Remove from heat and let cool completely.
2. Juice 3 to 4 limes and set aside lime juice.
3. Take 6 mint leaves and muddle them in the bottom of glass. You can use a wooden spoon, or the other end of a butter knife (especially if you are feeling more stressed than usual after that day's news report).
4. Add ice to glass. Next add in the simple syrup and lime juice. Then add rum topped with seltzer. Garnish with 2 mint leaves and serve with a straw. Enjoy!

Submitted by: Anonymous

"It's simply a rumor, everybody! I am not running for anything except for the impeachment of Trump!" - Congresswoman Maxine Waters, *The View*, August 4, 2017.

NASTY WOMAN

Serves 1

INGREDIENTS

- 2 oz gin
- 1/2 oz orange curacao or orange liqueur (such as Cointreau or Grand Marnier)
- 1/2 oz jalapeno pickle liquid (such as Trader Joe's brand) or liquid from the hot pepper version of Don's Small Pickles
- 2 TB of pasteurized egg white or 1 white of one large fresh egg if you like to live dangerously

DIRECTIONS

1. Place all ingredients WITHOUT ICE into your cocktail shaker. Shake vigorously until frothy.

2. Add ice to the shaker and shake vigorously again to chill.
3. Pour into a coupe glass and garnish with a jalapeno pickle slice.

CONTRIBUTOR NOTES

This cocktail is based on the classic White Lady, replacing the lemon juice with hot pickle juice for a spicier and nastier cocktail. The initial "dry shake" without ice will give you a frothier result.

Submitted by: Joan Berglund

"I am a nasty woman…. I'm not as nasty as a man who looks like he bathes in Cheetos dust. A man whose words are a distraction to America; Electoral College-sanctioned hate speech contaminating this national anthem…. I'm nasty like the battles my grandmothers fought to get me into that voting booth." - "Nasty Woman" poem by Nina Donovan, read by Ashley Judd at the Woman's March, January 20, 2017.

BLOOD ORANGE IMPEACH-MINT

INGREDIENTS

Serves 6

Drink

- 1 1/2 C Mint Simple Syrup (see below)
- 1 C peach flavored vodka (Absolut Apeach Vodka is one brand)
- 1 C blood orange Italian soda

Mint simple syrup

- 1 C sugar
- 1 C water
- 1 C fresh mint leaves, packed tightly

DIRECTIONS

Mint simple syrup

1. Mix sugar, water, and mint leaves in a medium saucepan and bring to a boil.
2. Lower heat and simmer for 5 minutes until sugar is dissolved, stirring as needed.
3. Refrigerate until cooled.
4. Strain while (therapeutically) squeezing as much minty syrup as possible out of the leaves.

Drink

1. Chill ingredients.
2. Fill 6 collins glasses with ice cubes and 3 or 4 fresh firm peach slices.
3. Divide the drink ingredients among your glasses.
4. Garnish with a mint sprig and an orange peel twist.

Submitted by: Irene Rea

"In 2008 - less than ten years ago - Trump appeared on the radio show and told Stern the story of an elderly man falling and subsequently bleeding profusely at a Red Cross charity ball at his Florida Mar-A-Lago resort. 'So what happens is, this guy falls off (the stage) right on his face, hits his head and I thought he died. And you know what I did? I said, 'Oh, my god, that's disgusting,' and I turned away... He's bleeding all over the place, I felt terrible, you know. Beautiful marble floor, it didn't look so good...I was saying, 'Get that blood cleaned up, it's disgusting.'" - Caleb R. Newton, "Elderly Man Falls At Mar-a-Lago; Trump Complains About Blood Staining Marble Floor," *BipartisanReport.com*, September 28, 2017.

SNOWFLAKE SESSIONS' WHITEST MINT JULEP

Makes 1 serving

INGREDIENTS

- 2 oz white dog whiskey or white moonshine
- 1/2 oz simple syrup or 1/4 oz agave syrup
- 8 mint leaves
- Mint sprig for garnish

DIRECTIONS

1. Muddle the mint and syrup in a 12 oz mason jar.
2. Add the liquor.
3. Add crushed ice and stir until the outside of the jar turns frosty.

CONTRIBUTOR NOTES

Unaged whiskey or sour mash liquor sounds scary, but they are generally put out by craft distilleries using high-quality ingredients and recipes. The practice of releasing some of the batch right away originated because some of the smallest companies just couldn't afford to sit on their whole batch while it aged. New England is home to a number of craft distilleries, so there are some good local choices.

Submitted by: Joan Berglund

"I'm not able to be rushed this fast. It makes me nervous." - Attorney General Jeff Sessions to Senator Kamala Harris during a Senate Intelligence Committee hearing on Russia, June 13, 2017.

"They are terrified of black women. Whenever a black woman says something about this administration, they're quaking in their boots." - Jason Johnson on *All in with Chris Hayes*, September 13, 2017.

TOTAL ECLIPSE TRAVEL TEQUILA MOONRISE

(On the Taxpayer's Dime)

Makes 1 serving

INGREDIENTS

- 1 1/2 oz tequila
- 4 to 6 oz grapefruit juice
- 1/2 oz blue curacao

DIRECTIONS

1. Add the tequila and grapefruit juice to a highball glass.

2. Drizzle the blue curacao over the top.

Submitted by: Joan Berglund

"[Steven Mnuchin's] comments Thursday about the jet travel aren't going to help put this to bed. 'You know, people in Kentucky took this stuff very serious. Being a New Yorker and [living for a time in] California, I was like, the eclipse? Really? I don't have any interest in watching the eclipse.' It's hard to read his comments as anything but demeaning to the people of flyover country. Those people were interested in the natural phenomenon, he seemed to be saying, but as a metropolitan man who has lived on both coasts, it just wasn't that interesting to me." - Aaron Blake, "Steve Mnuchin's tone-deaf response to his government plane controversy," *WashingtonPost.com*, September 15, 2017.

THIS DOG-GONE ADMINISTRATION IS A CAT-ASTROPHE

FROSTY PAWS

INGREDIENTS

- 32 oz vanilla yogurt
- 2 TB peanut butter
- 2 TB honey
- 1 large jar of baby food fruit or 1 mashed banana

DIRECTIONS

1. Mix up the ingredients.
2. Spoon into ice cube tray.
3. Freeze.

Submitted by: Elizabeth Lewis

"Barack Obama made a lot of promises during his election campaign, but none more important than the one he made to his young daughters…And as he stood before the country as president-elect Tuesday, he announced that America would have a new First Dog come January." - Stacy St. Clair, "Obama promises daughters a puppy in the White House," *ChicagoTribune.com*, November 5, 2018.

"Of all the stains besmirching the Trump presidency —the ethical lacunae, the spasmodic 'policy' fits, the Golf Digest aesthetic— none looms so large as the absence of a White House pet. Breathes there a man with a soul so dead that he doesn't want a loyal dog or faithful feline trotting beside him when he mounts that lonely staircase to the venerable Master Bedroom? Apparently yes." - Alex Beam, "What Kind of Pet Should Donald Trump Get?" Opinion, *NYTime.com*, April 15, 2017.

HOLY MACKEREL

INGREDIENTS

- 15 oz can of jack mackerel fish
- Flour
- 2 tsp salt
- 1 tsp baking powder
- Garlic powder

DIRECTIONS

1. Mix together everything, INCLUDING the water from the fish can.
2. Mix in enough flour for texture.
3. Spread out on cookie sheet and score into sections.
4. Bake at 350 degrees Fahrenheit for 30 min or until golden brown.
5. Store in refrigerator or freeze.

Submitted by: Elizabeth Lewis

"Bo has a new best friend in the White House. President Obama and his family took in a second Portuguese Water Dog named Sunny, an adorable addition who will serve as a playmate and 'little sister' to First Dog Bo, according to the White House's official website." - Corinne Lestch, "Bo Obama gets a playmate! Obamas adopt another dog," *NYDailyNews.com*, August 19, 2013.

LAPDOG RYAN DOG TREATS

Makes about 10 treats

INGREDIENTS

- 1/2 C flour
- 1/2 C graham cracker, crushed
- 1 1/2 TB water
- 1/2 C rolled oats
- 1 egg

- 1 TB shredded cheddar cheese
- 1 tsp chicken bouillon granules [onion and garlic free]
- 1 T. peanut butter

DIRECTIONS

1. Preheat oven to 350 degrees Fahrenheit.
2. In a medium bowl, stir together flour, graham cracker, oatmeal, bouillon and grated cheese.
3. Stir in the water, egg and peanut butter. Add flour as necessary to make a stiff dough.
4. Spoon dough onto greased cookie sheet or roll out to make cut-outs.
5. Bake in preheated oven for 16 minutes. Cool before serving.

Submitted by: Jodi Muerhoff

"His comments are not anywhere in keeping with our party's principles and values," [House Speaker Paul] Ryan said in the [leaked 2016 audio] recording.... I am not going to defend Donald Trump - not now, not in the future." - Scott Bixby, "Breitbart Leaks Audio of Paul Ryan Dumping Donald Trump," *TheDailyBeast.com*, March 13, 2017.

"I think the president is giving us the leadership we need to get the country back on the right track." - Paul Ryan to Sean Hannity, @FoxNews, *Twitter.com*, September 27, 2017.

SWEET APPLE PAWTATO PUPCAKES

Yields 12 regular size "Pupcakes"

INGREDIENTS

Pupcakes

- 3/4 C garbanzo bean flour
- 1 C all-natural sweet potato, pureed
- 1 small apple, finely grated
- 1/2 C unsweetened applesauce
- 1 large egg, beaten
- 1 TB raw honey
- 1 TB coconut oil

Icing

- 2 oz cream cheese
- 2 TB unsweetened applesauce

DIRECTIONS

1. Preheat the oven to 350 degrees Fahrenheit.
2. In a large bowl, combine the pureed sweet potato, grated apple, applesauce, honey and coconut oil until well mixed.
3. Pour in the beaten egg, stirring until incorporated then add the garbanzo bean flour.
4. Once the dough comes together, grease your cupcake pan and slowly spoon the batter in until 2/3 full.
5. Bake for 20-25 minutes, or until an inserted fork comes out clean.
6. While the Pupcakes are cooling, mix the cream cheese and applesauce in a bowl with a hand mixer until it is smooth and set aside.
7. Once the cakes are cool, dip the tops in the icing mixture.

CONTRIBUTOR NOTES

If the icing is a little bit runny, add a little bit more cream cheese to thicken. You can also put the Pupcakes in the refrigerator for the icing to harden before serving and it is made from all natural and healthy ingredients for your beloved canine companions. Recipe can also be modified to make mini-sized Pupcakes for dogs on a diet.

I have a 6 year old yellow labradorable guide dog, and this is her favorite birthday treat every year! She is a raw fed carnivore, but even she needs sweet and indulgent treats once in a while to keep her spirits up in these trying times. :)

Submitted by: Minh Ha

"US First Lady Michelle Obama has shared a video of her 'taking it all in' as she walks through the White House for one of the final times. The video, posted on Instagram, shows Obama calling her two dogs as she strolls through the halls of the place she has called home for the last eight years." - Harriet Sinclair, "Michelle Obama shares heartwarming video of 'one last walk' through White House with her dogs," *IBTimes.co.uk*, January 19, 2017.

About Us

Action Together Massachusetts (ATMA) is a women-founded and women-led organization working to support and strengthen the ideals of American democracy. Our goal is to create a politically and socially engaged community that holds itself, elected officials, and institutions accountable for fulfilling the promise of our diverse, democratic nation.

To achieve this, we provide and encourage a variety of civic and legislative actions, connect members with events, resources and training opportunities, establish regular contacts with legislators and other decision makers, and work in all ways to ensure our collective voices are heard from the workplace to the halls of Congress.

The ATMA network includes nine regional groups that span the Commonwealth of Massachusetts as well as a statewide group that includes members from each region.

Across our regional groups, ATMA's work is centered on four priorities:

- *Connect* and share as a community
- *Network* to build partnerships and alliances with each other, existing progressive groups, and our local, state and national legislators
- *Learn* about issues, legislation and opportunities for action
- *Act* in order to make a real impact and improve our Commonwealth and our nation

In all areas, ATMA stands for equal rights, religious tolerance, freedom of the press, science, inclusivity, social justice, economic freedom, and fundamental human decency.

INDEX

A

Alcoholic Beverages
    Bittersweet Orange Russian, 148
    Blood Orange, Peach, Mint, Mojito, 151
    Gin and Egg White Cocktail, 150
    Harvey Wallbanger, 146
    Mint Julep, 153
    Peach Mint Mojito, 149
    Tequila Moonrise, 154
    Vin Chaud, 145
Apples
    Apple Potato Pupcakes (Pet Treats), 161
    Cranapple Bars, 115
    Mulled Apple Cider, 142
    Waldorf Salad, 36

B

Bacon
    Green Salad, 30
    Meat and Bean Chili, 57
    Potato Salad, 31
    Roast Pork with Sausage Stuffing and Cherry Reduction, 52
Baked Brie in Puff Pastry, 8
Bananas
    Frosty Paws (Pet Treats), 157
    Smoothie, with Spinach, 140
Beef
    Meat and Bean Chili, 57
    Minestrone, 21
    Ribs, 78
    Roast, 60

    Steak Tips, 90
    Tacos, 59
Berries
    Beet Cake with Cream Cheese Frosting, 132
    Berry Juice Gel Mold, 130
    Berry No-Bake Pie, 114
    Blueberry Cake, 106
    Chocolate Coffee Trifle, Vegan, 102
    Cranapple Bars, 115
    Cranberries and Goat Cheese Stuffed Celery, 16
    Cranberry and Pecan Scones, 122
    Lemon Berry Sorbet, 97
    Pancakes, 72
    Rainbow Salad, 39
Bread(s)
    Cranberry and Pecan Scones, 122
    Garlic, 43
    Maple Cornbread, 33
    Monkey, 95
    Pancakes, 72
    Sausage Cornbread Stuffing, 52

C

Cake
    Apple Potato Pupcakes (Pet Treats), 161
    Beet, with Cream Cheese Frosting, 132
    Blueberry, 106
    Chocolate, 104
    Chocolate Coffee Trifle, 100
    Chocolate Coffee Trifle, Vegan, 102

ix

Granola, 10

I

Ice Cream
  Lemon Berry Sorbet, 97
  Neopolitan Icebox Cake, 96

K

Kale
  Garden Salad, 42
  Kale Chips, 15
  Vegetable Broth, 18

L

Lettuce
  Beef Tacos, 59
  Fried Chicken with Noodles
    and Watermelon Salad,
    80
  Herbed Pea Salad, 40
  Tabouli Salad, 35
  Vegetable Broth, 18

M

Mango
  Lassi, 138
  Salsa, 14
Meat. *See* Bacon, Beef,
  Chicken, Pork, Sausage
  Baloney Sandwich, 85
Mushrooms
  Chowder, Vegan, 23
  Savory Strudel, 70
  Vegetable Broth, 18

N

Nuts

Almond Bars, 99
Beet Cake with Cream
  Cheese Frosting, 132
Chocolate Chip Nut Cookies,
  118
Chocolate Nut Coconut Bars,
  127
Cranberries and Goat Cheese
  Stuffed Celery, 16
Cranberry and Pecan Scones,
  122
Garden Salad, 42
Squash Alfredo with Cashew
  Cream Sauce, 76
Wine Biscuits, 122

O

Oats
  Dog Treats (Pet Treats), 159
  Granola, 10
OLV
  Almond Bars, 99
  Baked Brie in Puff Pastry, 8
  Beet Cake with Cream
    Cheese Frosting, 132
  Berry No-Bake Pie, 114
  Blueberry Cake, 106
  Caramel Chocolate Chip
    Brownies, 125
  Chocolate Cake, 104
  Chocolate Chip Nut Cookies,
    118
  Chocolate Coffee Trifle, 100
  Chocolate Nut Coconut Bars,
    127
  Chocolate Pie, 107
  Coconut Flake Cookies, 113
  Cranapple Bars, 115
  Cranberries and Goat Cheese
    Stuffed Celery, 16

P

R

W

Y

CPSIA information can be obtained
at www.ICGtesting.com
Printed in the USA
LVHW02s0044130718
583621LV00011B/44/P

9 780999 723180